Growing Up in Bethlehem

a dusty little town can change your life forever

RICK BRITTAIN

DEDICATION

To the people of *First Baptist Church,*
Belen, NM on the occasion of her 100th anniversary.
What was
What is
What is to come

CONTENTS

ACKNOWLEDGMENTS

First, I want to thank Jesus, who gave me life and all the good things in it, including all of the following:

Thanks to my author friends Judy Edwards and Tim White for your correction and wisdom. I still don't know what I'm doing.

Thanks to the many friends, relatives, co-workers and the folks in all the churches who have shared your lives with me. Isn't it good that God lets us walk the journey together?

Thanks to the people in the chapters of this book who have taught me so much, and allowed me to share part of your story. I am the proud owner of a long list of heroes.

Thanks to Bob and Judy Brittain, who also gave me life, and taught me how to live it. My love and appreciation for you is reflected on every page of this book. You got me ready to leave, and for that I am forever grateful. The arrow loves the bow.

To my brothers, Mike and Dave, and their families. I am honored to share your name, life, and DNA. Aim small.

To my daughters Haylee, Mattie and Sydney, and my son-in-law Phillip. You all cause me to struggle with the sin called pride. I love you so much, and I am grateful to God for providing you for the good of this world. You know who we are, and you know what we do – FHL.

Finally, to Kris… my love, my partner, my wife. Thanks for encouraging me to write. It took a couple of decades to get started, I hope you like it! "We" is so much better than "I" could ever have been. Thanks for your patient love, your hard work, for going fishing with me, and for making our home a disciple-factory. I'd be glad to do this with you for a thousand years!

INTRODUCTION

It was a dusty little town in the middle of nowhere. The nearest large city wasn't too far away in miles, but a long way off in some other ways. Important people didn't come to Bethlehem, and as a rule, not many from Bethlehem became important.

There were a couple. A local sheep-rancher named Jesse had a son who gained a lot of notoriety in politics. Another time the wife of a carpenter from up north had a baby while visiting in town. That kid became the most important figure in the history of mankind. You know.

Because of that child, towns all over the world have been named after Bethlehem... towns in many countries, named in many languages. In Spanish, which is widely used in my home state of New Mexico, Bethlehem is translated "Belen."

A lot of people would say Belen is a dusty little town in the middle of nowhere. There's a pretty large city nearby, which is also far off in some ways. And like the other Bethlehem, important people don't tend to come there.

1

But sometimes a skinny sixth grader will move into a town like Belen, unaware that a dusty little town can change your life forever, and make you who you will be.

It was January when I arrived in Belen, sprawled in the back of a station wagon, asleep in a pile of luggage. As I remember, we arrived early in the morning, which is a strange time of day to finish a long trip. I can't remember why I was riding with someone besides my family, but I was.

I felt the car brake, heard voices and the sounds of arriving, and decided to take a look. The first thing I saw was the yellow-brown metal building that would host some of my best and worst moments over the next ten years. But that day, it was just a yellow-brown metal building.

The gaze shifted right, and rested on a squatty little block house, surrounded by a uselessly short chain-link fence. Further right there was a two-story building made of brick and some dirt-colored stuff I would learn to call *stucco*.

The station wagon's hatch opened and I crawled out to complete my survey. The vacant lot across the street looked good for football, and the words "Let's Go Bowling!" on the side of next building grabbed my full attention (I liked bowling – still do).

I walked up on the sidewalk and said hi to my parents and brothers. It seemed the squatty block house was where we would live, so I headed inside to find the bathroom. I guess that house would have looked pretty sad next to our beautiful two-story home back in South Carolina; but when you're eleven and male, you don't waste much time thinking about unimportant things like houses. I was hungry.

You see, I was a kid –all the way through. And I'd been a fortunate kid so far. By the grace of God, I was born in New Mexico, a treasure for which I will always be thankful. At about 6 years old, I'd arrived on a massive ranch in North Texas: endless woods; seven, *seven*! ponds; fishing, turtles, frogs, crawdads and lots of other critters. We raised chickens and fought over them with the coyotes. I adopted the only cat I ever loved, got a set of stitches in my head, and learned to hate snakes - Kid Paradise.

Then we moved. Florida. The beach. We lived on the East coast of the Sunshine State for a couple of years: body surfing, sandcastles, alligators, a whole ocean to fish in. I got some crazy sunburns, fell in love with the Chevy Camaro, scored a second set of stitches in the head, and developed a taste for wild pig - Kid Paradise.

Another move. South Carolina. We lived on a huge wooded lot with a million trees, a creek flowing through the back yard, and epic skateboarding hills. Dad would take me for long rides up the Blue Ridge Parkway on his motorcycle, and I learned to crash a mini-bike in the vacant lot across the street from our church. And yes, I picked up a third set of stitches...in my head – Kid Paradise.

Belen in winter didn't seem to hold much promise as a kid paradise right at the start. That vacant lot set the tone for the whole town. It was dry, rough, and plain. No trees, no plants, no water...nothing. It would be fine for football, but without the football you'd be a bored kid.

Belen looked like the kind of place where you'd better bring your own fun if you *didn't* want to be a bored kid.

A few days later the kid showed up at Central School. Did I mention how great it is to move 2,000 miles and drop into a new school half way through your sixth-grade year? Not great at all.

The new school was different. Most of the kids were a little browner than me and had strange last names like Baca and Martinez and Jaramillo (the J sounds like an H). My first lunch featured something that looked a little like Salisbury steak. A couple of the guys assured me it was horse meat, and I wasn't sure they were lying. I'm still not.

I met my first bully that day – I guess I'd been lucky up to now. He called me a name in Spanish, and let me know that if I looked at his girlfriend he'd kick my gringo... well, you know. I figure by the end of sixth grade I'd heard more cuss words in Spanish than I had in English. A well-rounded education.

It's funny. I can't remember that bully's name, though we went to school together for the next six years. I do remember the names of some other kids, though - kids that became friends. One would be best man at my wedding.

As I mentioned before, Belen was a dusty little town when I got there. It still is. It's the kind of place where you have to dig a little. They say if you can make it in New York, you can make it anywhere. I never could figure out what was so tough about a place that has everything. Belen had a whole lot of nothing. Try making it in a place like that.

I think that's why God chose Israel's greatest King from that other Bethlehem, and why He chose to have his son born there. The Bible says it like this,

Bethlehem Ephrathah, you are small among the clans of Judah; One will come from you to be ruler over Israel for Me. His origin is from antiquity, from eternity. Micah 5:2

Bethlehem wasn't much when King David grew up there, and it still wasn't much when Jesus got there; but it became a pretty important place because of who it produced.

My Bethlehem wasn't a kid paradise when I got there; but the things that happened to me there – the people I knew there – are what makes it an important place to me. And looking back, I'd have to say it became about the best place this kid could be from.

1 THE CRISIS

Not long after we arrived in Belen, there was a crisis. The nature and extremity of the crisis can only be understood in light of the characters involved.

I had just turned eleven years old. My older brother, Mike, was thirteen; and little brother, David, was a tender eight-and-a-half. The crisis was a transportation crisis, and it was a mathematical crisis. There were three boys and two bicycles. To complicate matters, both bicycles had some flaws, and both were a little large for little David to ride.

In a town like Belen, a boy without a bike is like a bird without wings, a ship without a sail, a peanut without butter. Hopelessly incomplete. The crisis was quickly communicated to the solver of all problems... Dad.

Dad was good at everything. He could fix anything, and as far as we knew then, his omnipotence hovered somewhere below that of Jesus himself, and somewhere above that of the US Government. So the evening Dad called us out to explain his solution to the great bike crisis of 1978, we gathered with anticipation.

The decision had been made that the best parts of the two bikes would be combined, making a fine machine for son number one. Son number three – he was always spoiled – would be taken to whatever bike-selling store Belen had to offer to pick out a new ride.

"Now, go get ready for bed, I gotta work on the car."

Everyone scattered, and I stood there alone, trying to figure out what had just happened. I redid the math in my head over and over, but no matter how I figured it, there would still only be two bicycles, and none of them had my name on it. The crisis had just escalated.

I didn't know what to do. My stomach hurt. My eyes burned. My knees felt weak. "Dad knows what he's doing. He *always* knows what he's doing. For some reason, I don't get a bike. What did I do to deserve this?"

I drifted across the back yard and over to the side of the squatty block house. My back slid down the wall and I hit the ground in a puddle. The tears came in a flood. No bike. The implications crowded my mind. "Why?"

As I sat there sobbing, I heard my Dad's voice. "Ricky? Hey buddy, what's wrong."

"I (sob) don't (sob) understand (double sob, with a string of snot) why I don't get (sob, deep breath, sob) a bike!"

My Dad's puzzled face looked down at mine. After a moment, he answered. "You do get a bike. You're going to get to pick one out at the store, just like David. Ok?"

"Ok? OK?! Are you kidding me? Dad, you're about to give me a heart attack! I'm going to lose my hair in my late thirties because of what just happened here! This is why middle children end up in therapy! OK?????" Actually, I didn't say any of that. Didn't even think it. You know what I thought?

"KID PARADISE!" Wonder of wonders! A new bike.

In a moment, in the twinkling of an eye, everything changed. It was just a misunderstanding, Dad explained later. That was the plan all along. Of course I would have a bike. A kid without a bike is like a ship without a... well, you know.

The Folks took us to the store and there was a whole row of bikes just begging to be put into service by a slick young explorer like me.

David picked out an orange kid-looking thing with a banana seat and pedal brakes. My tastes were more sophisticated. I selected a green ten-speed – bright green, and as cool as the other side of the pillow. That green beauty and I covered a whole lot of Belen together over the next few years.

Crisis averted, order restored.

That night when I sat alone behind the squatty block house is burned in my mind for two reasons. First, because in a town like Belen, a kid without a bike is hopelessly incomplete.

And second, because my Dad came through for me… which is a pretty important thing to a kid. You see, God created Dads to come through for their kids. That's the job. It's the work and the reward all at once.

Coming through means a lot of different things for a Dad:

It means working hard to meet your family's needs.

It means loving a kid's Mom more than you love the kid… so the kid will always know security at home.

It means cheering your kid on to greatness, no matter how little or how great their greatness may be.

It means teaching a boy how to fix a car, work a computer or love a woman.

It means rubbing some dirt on that skinned knee and helping your kid get up and try again.

Coming through means holding your daughter tight after her heart has been broken, and letting her know there is a man who will always be there. And it means teaching her what a man really is, so she'll know one when she sees him.

Coming through means teaching your child how to live by faith… how to believe God more than you believe hard times or hard people.

One of my favorite scriptures is called the *Shema*. Shema is a Hebrew word, and it means "listen."

Listen, Israel: The Lord our God, the Lord is One.
Love the Lord your God with all your heart,
with all your soul,
and with all your strength.
These words that I am giving you today are to be in your heart.
Repeat them to your children. Talk about them when you sit in your
house and when you walk along the road,
When you lie down and when you get up.
Bind them as a sign on your hand and let them be a symbol on your
forehead.
Write them on the doorposts of your house and on your gates.
Deut 6:4-9

Look at it. Do you see a Dad in there? I do.

Repeat them to your children. Whose job is it to teach the scripture to a kid? Believe it or not, the Bible indicates it is a Dad's job. Not the Sunday School teacher. Not the youth pastor. Not even the preacher. And please don't miss this – not just the Mom. The first responsibility and the first honor here belongs to the father. He sets the tone, and just like the guy who gave us bikes, he comes through.

"But how?" Good question. Keep reading.

Talk about them when you sit in your house and when you walk
along the road, when you lie down and when you get up. The great thing Dad did for us – maybe the greatest thing - was that he took us with him. He took us hunting and fishing and riding motorcycles and running and all the fun stuff.

But he also took us with him to the shop when it was time to build a shelf or fix a leak. He took us with him when it was time to add a room onto the house or buy a car.

He also took us with him when it was time to tell somebody about Jesus, or speak at a youth rally, or maybe visit a hospital.

He invited us into his life.

The night I asked Jesus to be *my* God was one of those inviting times. Dad was asked to speak to the football team at Pilot Point High school in North Texas. I heard him explain to the young men that Jesus loved them and wanted them, but that they *needed* Him. They needed forgiveness and a new start. They needed wisdom and power. They needed *life*.

After the talk was over, and we climbed back into Dad's pickup, I asked him some questions. He answered them. We talked for a while, and I gave myself to Jesus. Then I spent the rest of my childhood and young-adult years learning from Dad and Mom what it means to be a disciple.

Now that I'm a Dad, and my kids are leaving the nest, I can tell you from both sides – as a kid and as a Dad – that there's nothing better than parents teaching their kids how to live and love and work and grow... teaching them to *Love the Lord, your God with all your heart, all your mind and all your strength.* There's nothing like coming through for your kids, then watching them come through, too.

And there's no better way to do that than to invite them into your life. Take them along. Teach them to do what you love to do, and help them find what they love to do.

And by all means – get them a bike.

2 THE COWBOY

Tonka was a hard-headed old mare. White as snow where she hadn't started to yellow, and rightly named for those hard toy trucks I used to play with. I don't remember Tonka for any other reason than that she was the first horse Stan Henderson ever put me on.

Stan was a cowboy. I won't bore you here with a long explanation of what it means to be a cowboy, and I'm afraid lots of people have a misunderstanding of the word, but it is one of those words that you either get or you don't. They say Louis Armstrong was once asked to define rhythm. Louis replied, "well, if you got it you don't need no definition; and if you ain't got it, ain't no definition gonna help."

That's kind of how it is with a word like cowboy. It is a way of life more than a job, and it impacts everything you do.

Now, I've been a nut for cowboys all my life. I grew up in

the home of a cowboy, and all my favorite movies are about cowboys (who have lived in many places and at many times, if you know what I mean). So when I met Stan, I immediately knew this was a guy I wanted to be around. He had an air about him. Confidence. Control. And joy. Later, I'd see Stan do magic with a horse, and with a bunch of young men, too. But that was later. All I knew was that I liked this guy from the start, and I wanted him to like me.

When Stan put me on that old hag, he said one simple thing, "Make sure she knows who's in charge, and you'll be fine."

Well, there it was. If I wanted to impress the cowboy, I was gonna have to handle her. So off we went. I had a ball that day, and I don't remember any particular problems handling Tonka. Looking back, she wasn't too rough.

At the end of the ride, Stan asked me how it went.

"Fine."

"Good job."

And that was it. I hadn't embarrassed myself, and Stan had spoken kindly to me. Good day.

Over the next few years, I spent a lot of time with Stan Henderson. Including the time he showed me how to gentle a horse.

My Dad bought me a little red-roan gelding named Twister, who was about two when we got him. Twister had never been trained at all, never had a person on his back. He was gentle, and had been around people a lot, but never ridden or saddled, or even bridled.

Stan took me down to a pen where Twister was standing alone, and started showing me how to get to know a horse. Before long, I was sitting on that horse's back. He never bucked me a single time... not that day or ever after. You see, Stan understood horses, and he understood boys, and he brought the two together and left me feeling like I was the hero in this story.

We hunted together, too. We shot pheasants and ducks and doves. Don't tell my Dad, but Stan was the one who really helped me figure out how to handle a shotgun. The hunt I remember, though, was a deer hunt. We were on horseback in the Pecos wilderness, and it was cold.

There was about six inches of snow on the ground, and in the trees. We all paired up to go out hunting, and Stan took me, which was more than fine. He told me to stay right behind him, be quiet and keep my eyes open, so I did.

Moving through the thick timber, a problem developed. Every time Stan passed a tree and brushed a branch, the branch would swing back, and all the snow on it would land in my lap or on my leg.

I know what you're thinking. "Why didn't you fall back a little bit?" Good question.

Answer: Because Stan Henderson said to stay right behind him. As a twelve-year-old boy, riding with a hero, I didn't feel I had the right to edit the plan, so there I stayed.

After about a week of riding and shivering, Stan decided it was time to stop and eat something. I crawled out of the saddle and hit the ground like a block of ice. Stan looked over at me and asked if I was alright.

"I'm kinda cold. My pants got a little wet from the snow."

"How'd you get all the snow on you?"

"From the trees you kept hitting."

He grinned. "Why didn't you drop back a little?"

"'Cuz you told me to stay right behind you."

The grin faded and he got a serious look on his face. "Well, let's build a fire and peel those Wranglers off you and dry out."

Which he proceeded to do. Stan got the fire going while I lost the Wranglers and the long Johns I was wearing, along with my coat and shirt. I stood there in my shorts and t-shirt feeling a little foolish, but so tired and cold I just didn't care. We hung my clothes up and I huddled by that hatful of fire while Stan fixed me some beef stew from a can we'd brought.

That stew didn't stand a chance. I inhaled it and looked sadly at the empty can.

"You'd better eat this other can of soup," he says.

"That's yours."

"Aw, I'm not hungry. I ate too much breakfast anyway, and Brenda says I'm gettin' fat."

"O.K." And I ate some more beef stew. A favor to the fat guy.

The cabin looked great when we rode in that evening, and I never heard Stan mention those wet clothes to anybody.

There were other adventures on that trip. People got lost in the mountains, a horse died, and I met the most terrifying lawman that ever lived. But that's another story.

I had more adventures with Stan, too. But there's one more that'll make my point. The best moment I ever had with Stan Henderson wasn't any time he was teaching me something. It was the day he let me give him my hat.

Did you ever see *The Man from Snowy River?* Best movie ever. The hero is an Australian cowboy named Jim Craig. For me, Jim Craig was the movie version of who I wanted to be. He was tough and cool and had a hot girlfriend. He handled himself the way a cowboy should. He proved his manhood in hard circumstances. Then there was the sweet Australian accent. This guy had it all.

About the time I first saw the movie, my Dad got me a hat. It was a Stetson – beaver, medium brim. And wonder of wonders, it was the same color and style as the one Jim Craig wore.

I raced to the bathroom and locked the door. I turned on the bathtub faucet and filled the room with steam. In no time flat, I had a hat creased just like the one my hero wore.

That was a tasty hat. Everybody liked it. And I'm not

gonna lie to you… It looked great on me. This reality hit home the next time I rode with Stan. He commented on it. Said he liked my hat. Perfect.

In fact he said it about every time he saw me in it from then on. Pretty soon he was teasing me about how that was too nice a hat for a kid, and I'd better give it to him. He knew I loved the attention, and he knew we wore the same size hat, so it was a lot of fun for him.

It was fun for me too, until the day I heard he was moving away. Stan and Brenda Henderson had taken a different job in the ministry they worked for, and would be leaving Belen. We were all sad. They were sad, too. And I had a problem.

I loved Stan a whole lot. I wanted to thank him for all he'd done for me, but I was a poor kid from Belen who didn't have any money or any wisdom or anything else to give a guy like that. Then it hit me. I'd give him my hat.

So the next time I saw Stan, I wore the Stetson. I played it cool. "Hey Stan, you like this hat don't you."

He laughed. "Yeah, I do. But the thing is, Ricky, that hat likes me. It just looks better on my head than it does on yours."

I looked him right in the eye, and agreed. "Yeah. You're right. You'd better take it."

He was speechless for a second, then Stan said no. He wasn't the kind of guy to accept something so precious from a kid. But as I looked at him, tearing up just a little bit, he understood.

He understood that I needed to give him that hat, so he took it. He took it and thanked me and called me brother. Kid Paradise.

A few months later we went to visit Stan and Brenda, and when we pulled up at the ranch, he was wearing my hat. Perfect. We laughed about how good it looked on him, and all was right with the world.

The fourth chapter of Matthew's Gospel in the New Testament, tell us about a time when Jesus was walking along the shore of the lake of Gallilee, and he saw some young guys who had been out fishing. Now these guys had heard of Jesus. They knew he was a Rabbi who spoke with authority, and who performed miracles. What they didn't know was that Jesus viewed them the same way Stan Henderson viewed me: worthwhile.

Jesus looked at those guys and called them out. "Come, follow me, and from now on, you'll catch men." He called them out just like Stan called me out: over and over, further and further. He kept calling them out until the last day. He taught them and built them and trusted them.

And he did one more thing that Stan always did for me. He let them know they had a part to play in the story. He made them feel like they mattered. He made it about them instead of only about himself.

Have you ever thought about how often Jesus pulled his guys into the action when he could more easily have done it himself? He let them heal people and feed people and baptize people. He explained things to them that no one else got to understand. Jesus made men out of those twelve misfits, and then he handed the whole operation over to them. He trusted them with the birth and building of His Church.

Jesus called his disciples and trained them, and then he let them serve him – worship him. I see Jesus surrounded by those guys, declaring their love and devotion, promising to stick with him forever, going about the mission he gave them. I see them staying right behind him, doing it the right way, but also missing the point and messing up regularly. I see Jesus allowing his men to give back from what He gave them, and I can't help but think of that old hat.

Nowadays, I love investing in young men more than just about anything else I get to do. I love letting them know they have a part to play in Jesus' story. I love seeing them get it, and then give it away. Sometimes when I'm working with a young guy, I think of men like Stan who invested in me, and I realize they taught me something beautiful.

You see, Jesus had the twelve, and Paul had Timothy and a bunch of others. Barnabas had John Mark, and on and on it goes. Jesus' plan hinges on the older investing in the younger and the younger learning from the older.

In Paul's first letter to Timothy (see your new Testament), he opens with these words, "Paul, an apostle of Christ Jesus by the command of God our Savior and Christ Jesus our hope: to Timothy, my *true son in the faith.*"

Isn't that great? "My true son in the faith." They aren't

related by blood, but they are forever connected by Jesus. And the older guy draws the younger guy into the story, teaches him to live the life, and sends him out on a mission from God. That's how worlds get changed, and that's what men like Stan did for me.

Thanks, Cowboy.

3 THANK YOU, JESUS

Some of the people in Belen came from far away, and sometimes you could tell they just weren't from around there. Of all the people I knew in Belen, there was no more obvious out-of-towner than Momma Mott.

Lula Mae Mott was from Pittsburgh, PA, and you could tell she wasn't from Belen because of her skin. In all my years in Belen, I can only think of around 20 African-American people I knew in that town. Momma Mott was the first, and easily the most memorable.

Everyone called her Momma because that's what she told us to call her, and because it just fit. She loved kids more than anything else in the world except Jesus – who she loved more than you can imagine. More about that later.

When I met her, she must have been about nine feet tall. Over the years she shrank a little at a time, and ended up around five-foot-eight. She had the brightest eyes you ever saw, and they were always alive; with joy, or fire, or praise, or even pain. Sometimes her eyes were so intense I thought her face was going to burst.

Her face was old, but I don't remember wrinkles, and her hands were strong, but kind. Yeah, that actually describes just about all of her... strong, but kind.

Her fighting weight would have been well over 200. I say fighting weight because I am pretty sure she could have whipped anybody she wanted to, even in her seventies. In fact, Momma used to tell a story about the time she threatened Muhammad Ali – "the baddest in the world" - because his car was scaring the children in the Pittsburgh neighborhood where she served as a police officer. She told Ali to slow down or she would pull him out of that limousine and show him who was the *baddest in the world*. Ali told his driver to slow down.

That's how Momma Mott was. When she spoke, you listened. She made sure you listened. Some people (Like Ali) listened because she scared them into it. Some listened because her voice was so loud, and you couldn't really help but listen. Us kids listened because we loved her so much, and because you always wanted to hear what she was going to say.

I never saw Momma Mott hurt anybody on purpose... but when she grabbed you, it was sort of like being grabbed by the Pittsburgh Steelers. And she buried us all under the crushing weight of her love.

Momma's love was most often delivered in the form of one of her world-famous hugs. She'd see a kid coming down the church hallway and make her move. "Come here, baby!" It didn't matter whether you were six years old or six feet tall, everyone was "baby."

Sometimes she'd reach into her big purse and pull out a piece of hard candy. Just as your hand closed on the candy, she'd cut loose the pythons. Two muscled, ebony arms would envelop your whole body.

The hug would sometimes lift you off the ground, then the left hand would slide up to the back of your head and grab hold. Once she got a handful of hair, she'd make a fist. Then the moment of truth....

If she was particularly happy to see you, or just happy in general; she'd make her way around the side and *bite you on the ear.*

I am not making this up.

She bit people. She bit *me.* She bit my brothers. She bit a bunch of kids.

As an act of love.

And it worked! Once the initial shock and pain wore off, you found yourself hanging there in mid air; a skinny white kid just as grateful as can be that a huge black woman had just bitten you on the ear. Kid Paradise.

The hugs were awesome… in several ways. But the best moments were when she got happy.

I mentioned earlier that the only thing Momma Mott loved more than kids was Jesus. The love was on display when she sang and played the piano. She used to leave bruises on the white keys. To this day, *Life is Like a Mountain Railroad* is one of my favorite songs because of her… and I never hear it without seeing her in my mind's eye, banging away at that piano with her head thrown back and her eyes closed, singing her heart out to Jesus.

The love was visible when she talked about Jesus and when she cooked, when she gave you one of her hugs and when she told a story. But when Momma got happy, the love just poured out all over the place. It was like one of those Gatorade baths the winning coach gets at the end of a football game.

If you didn't grow up in the right kind of church, you probably don't know what it means to get happy. I hadn't ever seen it myself before moving to Belen.

Pastor Misener – educated, clean cut, dignified and wise – innocently teaching the scripture, would hear a small sound coming from his right, (second row – always) and he'd know what was coming next.

The beginning was a low moan, trailed by something along the lines of "mmmhmmm." Then words formed,

"Thank you Jesus, thank you Jesus."

"Oooohhhhhh, Praise Him!"

"Glory...glory!"

Pastor Misener would stop talking, and watch Momma Mott. I never knew what he was thinking, but I knew what I was thinking, and over the years, my thoughts progressed.

First, I thought she was having a fit. Then I thought it was funny because the sermon got interrupted. Next, I wondered why she did that. Sometimes I thought she was just being dramatic. Later, I wanted to know what *she* was thinking and how she got so excited. The last couple of times I saw Momma Mott get happy, I just hoped that someday – *someday* I would know a love for Jesus as strong as the one that inspired her.

After a minute or two, Momma Mott would quiet down, and sit down, and the shouts would fade into a slow, methodical, "thank You, Jesus," that made you want to thank Him, too.

In Second Samuel, Chapter six, there's a story about King David (kid from Bethlehem) entering Jerusalem with the Ark of the Covenant. The Bible says the whole host of Israel was rejoicing and that David danced before the Lord. From the Bible's description, I can only think David *got happy*.

Some people – including David's wife – didn't care for his getting happy. The Bible says that Michal "look down from her window and saw David dancing and leaping before the Lord, and she despised him in her heart." She was disappointed because her husband hadn't acted like a King. Her pride was hurt.

Michal's words reveal her heart, "How the king of Israel honored himself today! He exposed himself today in the sight of the slave girls of his subjects like a vulgar person would expose himself."

David's response reveals his heart, "I was dancing before the Lord who chose me... I will celebrate before the Lord, and I will humble myself. I will be honored by the slave girls you spoke about."

David entering Jerusalem in the company of the Ark of God was a singular moment of worship for the "man after God's own heart." It was a time when no one and nothing on earth mattered to the great king apart from the praise of the Great King.

David was "alone" with the Lord. All Israel was invited, and all Israel was in on the celebration... if they chose to be. But David had eyes and heart and mind only for his God. Just like Momma Mott when *she* got happy.

I'll never forget the first time Momma Mott pulled my hair during one of those hugs. It was joy and pain all rolled up together, and I'd give a whole lot to hug her right now, though there isn't much hair left to grab.

And I'll never forget seeing her get happy about Jesus.

One time I heard Momma Mott apologizing to our pastor after one of her happy episodes. "I'm sorry preacher. I try to be quiet, but sometimes I just can't help it."

Have you ever been so grateful to Jesus that you couldn't help it? If you have, you know what she and David knew.

If not, don't worry. There's still time.

4 BUCK FEVER

One of the best parts of being a country boy is the amount of time you get to spend "in the middle of nowhere." Growing up in Belen always seemed to lead me to a mountain, a river, a desert or a plain. I never had much trouble believing there is a God, and that He's good – largely because I saw so much of his best work.

One of the things we tended to do when we went to the middle of nowhere was deer hunting. We loved to hunt birds behind Mork, our trusty black lab; but deer hunting was special because it was such an event. Deer hunting meant traveling a few hours from home, camping out, cooking over an open fire, and riding horses over new country.

I guess I was about 14 the year we were invited to hunt the Lindsey ranch near Corona, New Mexico. Corona was the kind of town that made Belen look like a regular metropolis. It might not have been the middle of nowhere, but you could see it from there.

Corona was also known as excellent deer country, and I just knew this would be the year I got a chance at a buck. I'd been hunting deer for a couple of years, and never so much as shouldered my rifle to that point. It had mostly been snow and cold, and the vague idea that New Mexico actually contained live deer, which I might someday encounter during a hunt.

But this was my year, I just knew it. I'd practiced a bunch and felt good about hitting what I aimed at. I'd rehearsed my big shot hundreds of times in my mind. It would be spectacular. I was ready. I packed my gear, slid the Winchester behind the seat, and climbed into Dad's pickup.

Ah, the Winchester. It was a lever-action .30-.30. Looked just like the ones they carried in all those John Wayne movies we were always watching. It was a beautiful rifle, and it also fit my Dad's philosophy of kids and guns.

You see, Dad had a system. You started with single-shot weapons, because you needed to learn to hit your target the first time, instead of relying on repetition. I learned to shoot with a single-shot .22. My first shotgun was a single-shot .410. By my early teens, I'd moved up to a repeating rifle. The Winchester held five rounds.

The other part of Dad's philosophy was that scopes were for people who could already shoot effectively with open sites. I hadn't proved that level of expertise yet, so the Winchester carried no scope. No problem – I was John Wayne. Scopes are for old men and sissies, bring on the venison.

When we arrived at the ranch, we were shown to our room inside the house. I was sorely disappointed by the idea of sleeping indoors; then I found out we would be eating form a table inside a kitchen… the disappointments mounted.

Mrs. Lindsey managed to put together a fine dinner despite the limitations of indoor plumbing and a gas stove. We did a good job of getting rid of the evidence and sat down to visit for a while. Just as I settled into a chair, I heard the sound of a semi-truck pulling into the ranch yard. As any country boy can tell you, the sound of a truck like that usually means you'll be leaving your chair, which is exactly what happened. Dad looked over at me and smiled, then offered to help with whatever was in the truck.

It was a feed truck, loaded with 50-pound sacks of Calf Manna. You may not believe that I can really remember what kind of feed it was 35 years later. That's because you didn't help us unload that truck by hand. I handled enough Calf Manna that night to last me a lifetime. I had dreams about the stuff for three months.

Needless to say, I slept well that night – a great dinner and a little exhaustion will get you there - and woke up early ready to bag my deer. We hunted horseback the first day-and-a-half, saw a lot of country and a lot of sign. We felt good about our chances, but after lunch Dad decides we would cover a little more ground and do some sight-hunting from the truck. It was the warmest part of the day, and we didn't really expect to see anything, but at least we'd do some scouting.

As we rolled slowly down the dirt track, I scanned the hills right-left-right. While I scanned, I daydreamed about the deer I would bring down. Would he qualify for Boone and Crockett? Probably. Dad broke in on my dream with a press on the brake pedal and an announcement. "There he is."

I looked at Dad, then to the front. Left-right-left... hello! About a hundred yards ahead, just a stone's throw off the road, stood a beautiful mule deer – with antlers!

"Okay." Says my Dad. "Open your door *quietly*, and step away from the truck, then shoot him.

No problem. Never had a door been opened with more stealth and skill. As I slid from the seat, I tried to breath easily, and concentrate on the job at hand. Yeah, right.

I stepped off the road, staring at the deer, who calmly stared back at me. I guess he'd faced a fourteen-year-old with a .30-.30 Winchester before, because he seemed completely unconcerned by me and my gun. He'd obviously never seen a John Wayne movie.

I pulled the hammer back, shouldered the rifle, remembering my training, and sure I'd make this shot just like I'd done so many times before. I felt shaky and short of breath, but I pressed on. I sighted just behind the deer's shoulder, breathed in, let half the breath out, squeezed the trigger smoothly, and waited for him to drop.

He just kept staring at me. He might have winked, I'm still not sure. Something was wrong. My throat felt tight. My heart was pounding. I was shaking even more, and I

32

couldn't stop.

I levered the gun and threw it to my shoulder again. This time I didn't breathe or squeeze or any of that foolishness. I pulled the trigger like I meant it! And missed again.

As I was emptying the rifle, the sound must have gotten annoying, because the buck loped up the hill into the trees and left me standing there. I thought about throwing the Winchester at him – but I was pretty sure that would have been frowned on. It certainly wouldn't have been any less effective.

Buck fever.

I had just experienced my very own case of the hunter's most dreaded affliction. The strain had overcome me, and I had emptied my rifle without coming anywhere near the target. Whether you want to call it nerves, or panic, or adrenaline; the reality is that many beginning hunters experience it.

I've heard of grown men emptying a rifle without firing a shot... just levering shells onto the ground, with no idea what they're doing, or why. I've heard of people who simply *couldn't* pull the trigger. Buck fever is strange and humiliating, but it is also very real.

The funny thing about buck fever is that you never know if you're going to have it. Some people – like my annoying older brother – seem born to shoot. They have nerves of steel, ice-water in their veins, and a superior air that makes you want to kick them in the shin. They also tend to be fine hunters... but back to buck fever.

There simply isn't any way around it. The only way to get past buck fever is to go through it. You have to hunt, you have to shoot, and you have to deal with whatever comes. The good news is that for most people, once you've gone through it, you are able to move forward and hunt freely from then on. Buck fever is most often a once-in-a-lifetime terror.

I wonder how many people, if they knew they would experience buck fever, would simply pass on hunting altogether? How many would sacrifice the potential joy for the sake of missing the pain? It's one thing to look backward on buck fever and laugh. But what if you were looking forward at it?

It seems we humans are often dead-set against the concept of *through*. We're much more interested in around, or over or instead of. We want the reward without the pain, but if forced to choose, we'll just pass on both and take things as they are.

The passive life, however, is really no way to live. Jesus didn't think it was. One time, when the Master was teaching his men, Jesus said, *"You will have suffering in this world. Be courageous! I have conquered the world."* (John 16:33)

If you read the whole chapter, you'll find that Jesus is letting his guys know that big trouble is coming. They'll be hated, they'll be killed, they'll go through pain like a woman giving birth to a child, which I understand hurts quite a bit.

Jesus doesn't tell them that he'll keep them from suffering. He promises to keep them *through* their suffering. He promises some important things. First, Jesus promises to send His Holy Spirit, who he calls "the Comforter". The Spirit will guide, teach and strengthen Jesus' disciples, equipping us for all the trials of life.

Second, Jesus promises joy on the other side. He assures them that the trials are temporary, and the best days are coming. "Make no mistake, it will be worth it."

Finally, Jesus promises His peace. The beginning of verse 33, quoted above, says, "I have told you these things so that in Me you may have peace." It is important to remember that this peace is promised not only after the trial, but during the trial. Jesus guarantees life will be hard, but he also guarantees a way through and a great joy on the other side.

When I think back on that hunting trip, I remember some hard things, like unloading the feed truck, and missing my first chance at a deer. I also remember the ride home, when the horse trailer blew a tire on a lonely highway at two in the morning. We had to unload the horses and change the tire, which wouldn't have been so bad if the temperature had been above zero.

On the other hand, I remember being with Dad. I remember the second buck we saw, and the beautiful shot Dad made to bring it down. I remember him letting me follow the blood trail and find the deer by myself. I remember covering a lot of ground together and learning to think like a deer.

The reality is clear. Hard things are okay because they are the journey, not the end. None of us prefer the hard times, but they do teach us how to handle life, and they are temporary.

Besides, the end is worth so much. The book of Hebrews in the New Testament describes how Jesus, "for the joy that lay before Him endured a cross and despised the shame..."

He despised the shame.

Jesus knew what was coming, and knew that the shame of the cross wasn't even worth thinking on. He knew that "the joy set before Him" was so great that a little shame really didn't matter.

In this world, you will have trouble. But don't worry. Buck fever will pass, and the joy will come. And one of these days, Dad may let you use a scope!

5 THE ALL-STAR

You may recall that the first thing I saw when I arrived in
Bethlehem was a yellow-brown metal building. It sat next
door to the squatty block house that was our first home
there. Both the squatty block house and the yellow-brown
metal building were part of the church where my Dad
would work.

It was on that first day in Bethlehem that I discovered this
building was a kid paradise. They called it the South
Annex, because it was to the south of the main building.
It served as the church "fellowship hall" and housed the
kitchen, some classrooms, and – to my delight – a
basketball court!

That very day, I finagled access to the basketball court and
began a love affair with a yellow-brown metal building.
Actually, it was more a love-hate thing than a love affair.
It was there that I learned to dunk a basketball, spike a
volleyball, and flirt with a girl; but it was also there that I
had quite a few rough times.

Rough times can mean different things to different people, but for me, as a kid growing up in Belen, rough times usually meant an injury. I've already mentioned the three sets of stitches in my head. If I finish losing my hair one of these days, I'll probably bear a striking resemblance to Frankenstein's monster.

There were many more injuries over the years: countless rolled ankles – left and right, concussions (NFL players are whiners), broken fingers, two busted knees, a dislocated and rebuilt shoulder, and on and on. I was seeing a chiropractor for back problems when I was in junior high. I had growing pains in my knees, and my doctor told me I had rheumatoid arthritis and would be in a wheelchair before I finished college (he was wrong). I once spent an entire season on the Belen High School Cross-Country team and never ran in a meet… injuries. And in tenth grade I sprained my pancreas and have been an insulin-dependent type 1 diabetic ever since.

My greatest moment in the South annex, and my most spectacular injury, was the *Chariots of Fire* lean. The movie tells the story of Eric Liddell, who was a missionary to China and starred as a sprinter for Great Britain in the 1924 Olympic Games. In one scene, Liddell leans far forward to break the tape and win a race. This scene inspired me as a runner. I envisioned myself leaning to win like Eric Liddell. The problem was a simple one. I was too slow. My track career never included the breaking of any tape not wrapped around my own ankle.

But one Sunday night in the South Annex, we had a mini-olympics. There were lots of silly events, including a half-court foot race. Several of us took our places at one end of the basketball court, and the gun sounded. I got off to a great start and took the lead. As we neared half court (a good 30 feet from the starting line), I looked left and saw that my little brother (the one who was two years younger than me, but good at sports) was gaining quickly and it would be a photo finish.

This was it! My moment had arrived. I was Eric Lidell, about to bring home the gold for England. David was the American sprinter I must defeat for King and Country. As we crossed the line, I leaned far forward and claimed my victory (at least that's the way I remember it.) Then time stood still.

My victory lean put me off balance, and I began to stumble. I had less than forty feet to regain my balance and stop before I hit the wall someone had left way to close to the end of the basketball court. No deal.

Just as I gained my footing and got straightened up, the wall arrived. I threw my left hand out in front of me to try and slow the momentum. As the heel of my hand hit the wall, there was an audible snap, and a lot of pain. I bounced off the wall and grabbed my left wrist in my right hand.

I turned toward the onlookers and announced, "I broke my arm."

Because I was known as something of a wanna-be comedian, people must have thought I was joking. They laughed. This made me angry, so I proved it. I looked up at the amused crowd and uncovered my wrist. What those people saw may be burned in their minds to this day.

They saw the last two inches of my left forearm turned in a ninety-degree angle from the rest of it. There was some blood running down my wrist, and the white end of a bone peeked through the skin. The doctor later described my wrist as "swan-like" in appearance. It was quite beautiful.

I spent the summer before my senior year of high school with a cast stretching from my hand to near my shoulder, and pins holding my surgically repaired wrist together. By the end of that long summer, my arm was a noodle, the cast smelled worse than you can imagine, and my wrist and elbow were frozen in place. The only upside of the whole ordeal was the beautiful physical therapist I developed a crush on that fall.

Some of my sports injuries were simple accidents, and you can't really blame a guy for getting diabetes, stuff happens. But most of my problems were the result of trying to play sports with people who had the one thing I lacked... talent. I was never very fast or very strong or very quick. You never heard anyone say, "Boy that Brittain kid sure is *athletic*."

So I tried to make up for my lack of athleticism by a force of will and effort. I loved playing sports, and I wanted to be good at them. The obvious solution, to me, was to play with better players and try to keep up. The result of this strategy was that I spent much of my athletic career in a place called "out of control."

Out of control is a condition that leads to compound fractures, rebuilt shoulders and lots of rolled ankles. It's really no way to go through life. I just didn't know any other way to go. I still tend toward the out of control approach to sports. A few years ago when I was learning to ski, I took a half-day lesson from an instructor at the Santa Fe ski area. After my morning lesson, the instructor said, "You only have one problem, Rick."

"Yeah, what's that?"

"You aren't scared enough."

Perfect. My wife can confirm that this problem led to some earth-shaking and embarrassing antics on my returns to the slopes over the years. A lack of skill and a lack of fear are a dangerous combination!

But what if? What if I could have had some great basketball player or football coach, or alpine skier *connected to my brain* while I was muddling my way through all those sports. What if I could have had the mind of Larry Bird on the court or John Elway on the field? I'll bet I would have been an all-star.

Since I didn't have access to the mind of Larry Bird or John Elway, I stumbled through my teenage years tripping over my own feet while trying to compete with guys who actually had athletic talent. Sometimes it was painful, sometimes it was fun, and sometimes it got downright ugly. But what if?

Unlike my sports career, life with Jesus *does* come with that kind of help. In an amazing plot twist of power and kindness, God sent Himself to live in His people. In the very beginning of the book of Acts (1:8), Jesus promises his followers, *"You will receive power when the Holy Spirit has come on you, and you will be my witnesses..."*

If you spend some time in the book of Acts and the letters of Paul, you'll find that the Spirit of Christ comes to live in His disciples. The Spirit teaches us, corrects us, empowers us, directs our lives and blesses us with the constant presence of God. God gives us His Spirit so we can live the life He has created us to live. In a very real sense, He allows us to be all-stars.

The Christ-follower has the opportunity to live the "abundant" life Jesus came to give. There is the possibility of living with excellence in every way: how we treat people, how we make ethical decisions, how we choose our path in life, what we do with our relationships and our stuff. Because of the Spirit's presence, we are free.

Like most wonderful things in life, this one comes with a challenge. No one is forced by God to submit to His Spirit and receive His power. You see, the Bible teaches that the need to be filled with the Spirit is an ongoing thing. We need to be continually filled like a swimming pool in the desert. Every day, every hour, every interaction and every adventure is an opportunity to receive God's power, and to live on it. The journey never ends until heaven, so the need for the Spirit won't end either. Fortunately, the Spirit of Christ never runs out. He is forever and He is all-powerful.

Imagine a second-rate basketball player empowered with the mind of LeBron James. Oh, what possibilities. But better than that, imagine a run-of-the-mill kid from a dusty little town having access to the thoughts of God.

Who has known the Lord's mind that he may instruct Him? But we have the mind of Christ. (1 Cor. 2:16)

6 THE HIPPIE

Roger was the first hippie I ever knew. I'd seen them around and even met one or two, but Roger was a real person. He and his wife, Ann were part of our church in Belen… our token hippies. They had been real live, hard core hippies; but then they met Jesus, and set out to follow Him without selling out to the American Dream everyone else seemed to be chasing.

They were some of the kindest people I knew growing up, and they were really interesting to be around. They were interesting and fun because they were *different*. They didn't just march to the beat of their own drummer, Roger and Ann didn't march at all. They sort of ambled along at their own pace, wandering on and off the beaten path, for reasons known only to them. Roger was the kind of guy who would catch mice and rats around his place and save them for the neighbor up the road to feed to his South American Toad. 'Cuz why waste the rats, right?

Roger was a hairy guy. He had long hair – usually in a

pony tail – and an unruly beard cavorting around the lower half of his face. I don't know that Roger ever trimmed that beard, but it seemed to be changing shape all the time. He and Ann favored denim and leather, but not the kinds you'd find at the mall. They were sun-browned and rough-skinned. They worked hard, and made their own rules. And they welcomed us into their unique life and home.

The home was a sight to behold. We got to be around during construction, and my brother Mike actually worked for Roger, helping build it. The shop was completed first, and Roger and Ann lived in it while they built the house. It was big and open and all rough wood. It fit right into the sand and brush on the east side of the Rio Grande valley. I remember thinking, the first time I saw their place, that Roger had better not be planning on farming, because that spot hadn't grown anything more substantial than a sagebrush in a long, long time.

Back to the house. Roger had somehow gotten his hands onto a big naval buoy, and decided to make it the centerpiece of his house. It would be a fireplace, heating the entire home, which was to be built in a circle around it. There would be thick adobe walls, lots of glass, and passive solar heating for water. Come to think of it, I never heard the term "passive solar" before I met Roger, and probably not again for a long time after. To this day, the entire heating and cooling cost for that house is less than 500.00 a year.

There were a number of new words and concepts to be found when you spent time with Roger. He had a different way of looking at life, a unique set of priorities, and as I mentioned, a refusal to sell out to a way of life he didn't want. I had never met anybody who wanted to live out on the high desert, in a round house without any visible neighbors. I didn't understand why these people seemed to have an aversion to new things or stuff you could buy in stores. They were always excited about making their own stuff.

One of the new words I learned from Roger and Ann was "meningitis". They had a baby girl, and she got sick. I think that was the first time I was really aware of a very sick child, and it was frightening. I watched my folks and other people I loved and respected pray for Lisa – for her survival and her healing. As it turned out the sickness she developed was spinal meningitis, and though God did save her life, she lost her hearing. This led to lots of challenges and complications for their family, but what it didn't do was force them to become just like everybody else. Instead of being crippled by the challenge, the Swansons used it to make lives better. Their kids prove the point.

Lisa has a Master's degree in counseling from Gallaudet University and is the only deaf counsellor for the deaf in the state of New Mexico. How cool is that? Her sister Maia is a Craniosacral massage therapist. Part of her work involves putting patients in the water with dolphins. Don't ask me, I'm just the writer. I don't understand how any of this works, but it is beautiful.

I guess I've come to appreciate that, "not like everybody" approach more and more as the years go by. There are so many people in our world who are desperate to fit in, to be accepted as normal, though I'm not sure they know what normal means. I think what they're really striving for is something less than normal... let's call it *average*.

Normal is something entirely different. Average means you're just like everyone else. Normal means you are how you were meant to be. A normal computer turns on when you push the button, and doesn't crash. The average computer... well, you know what I mean.

I think Roger and Ann were pretty normal people. They lived toward Jesus, not toward everyone else in our town. They decided to be who they were, and follow the Master in that life.

I'm not saying there is anything particularly Christ-honoring about being a hippie; or a bricklayer or a bank teller for that matter. The key to the whole exercise is found in Paul's letter to the church in Galatia – in your Bible. Chapter one, verse 10 says, *"For am I now trying to win the favor of people, or God? Or am I striving to please people? If I were still trying to please people, I would not be a slave of Christ."*

The thing I liked about Roger was that he was very interested in pleasing Christ, but not too worried about pleasing everyone else. Because he was a hippie, this approach sort of stuck out all over him. And I liked it.

The other day, I was listening to one of my favorite songs by one of my favorite bands. The band was called DC Talk, and the song is called *Jesus Freak*. One part of that song is what reminded me of Roger and caused me to start writing this particular story. The song talks about another hippie who lived out on the desert, and didn't quite fit in with the crowd in town.

John the Baptizer – whose story you can find in all four of the Gospels in your New Testament - was a one-of-a-kind guy. The Bible says he was a "voice crying in the wilderness," telling everyone to "prepare the way for the Lord." John freaked people out, but he also got their attention. Huge crowds came to hear him speak and to repent for their sins, allowing John to baptize them.

John was a rock star. Then right at the height of his fame, he gave it all away to his cousin... who just happened to be the Son of God. Later, because he wouldn't keep his mouth shut, some powerful people had him executed by an immoral king.

What a crazy story! What a crazy guy! But Jesus himself declared that up to that time in human history, this wild man from the desert was the greatest human who had ever lived (Matthew 11:11). Chew on that. The greatest man who ever lived ate bugs.

You see, God has a different way of measuring value and success than our culture does. The things most people are so desperate for don't really matter to Him. The things most people don't have time for are often exactly what God is interested in. That's why freaks like John the Baptizer bring him so much joy. They have time for the things of God because they aren't wasting all their time on the things of the mall.

I've seen Jesus Freaks in many shapes, sizes and colors. They don't necessarily live in the wilderness, but they do live apart. They live apart from the pursuits that dominate and destroy so many lives. They keep their eyes on Jesus. They take seriously Jesus' command to seek first the

Kingdom of God and His righteousness (Matt 6:33). And they reap the reward of freedom every day of their lives.

I don't know if Roger reminds me of John the Baptizer, or if John reminds me of Roger, but I sure hope I remind somebody of guys like them.

7 MORE THAN MEETS THE EYE

One of the first people I met in Belen was the Pastor my
Dad would be working with. I really don't remember
anything about the day I met him, but I do remember a lot
about some other days we shared.

Milford Misener was a thoroughly middle-of-the-road
looking guy. Average height, average weight, and a little
border of short red hair surrounding the bald top of his
head. People called him "Red", which was a kindness... I
thought they should have called him "Clear".

I expected he would be nice, which he was; and I expected
him to be a good preacher, which he also was. I didn't
expect much else. In my eleven-year-old mind he was
ancient, nearly fifty. He would be another of the nameless
adults whose way a smart kid tried to stay out of.
Especially since he was the Pastor.

It didn't take long for my low-end expectations to be
shattered. I learned that very little of who Milford Misener

was, and how he operated, met my expectations.

First, there was basketball. Our church had that gym, and we lived in the squatty little block house that stood next to it. I spent as much of my time as I could in that gym, shooting baskets and honing my game.

One day, Pastor walked in and watched me for a couple of minutes. "Wanna play horse?" he asked. Uh-oh.

My mind raced. What should I say? I don't wanna play basketball with this old guy. If I beat him, I might get in trouble. If I lose...well that isn't happening. I saw no way out. Hopefully this wouldn't take long and I could get back to practicing.

"You go first," he said.

Sure. I'll take it easy on you. A free throw. Now I had been shooting about 200 free throws a day, and I rarely missed. I stepped to the line and sank one, then watched him retrieve the ball.

I was mildly surprised when he made the shot and smiled at me. No problem. I tried a twelve-footer from the wing and watched the ball clang off the rim. This might take a little longer than I thought.

The old man calmly walked to the top of the key and sank what would have been a college three pointer if we'd had three pointers in those days. Five shots later the game was over and he walked away counting my money.

Not really, there was no bet. But it felt like I'd just lost something. I decided I needed more practice. I also learned that my Pastor was athletic.

The next surprise was about football. I am a true blue (and orange) Denver Bronco fan. There is nothing a Bronco fan hates more than the Oakland Raiders. Imagine my shock when I found out this mild-mannered Man of God was a Raider fan. I didn't think Raider fans could even be Christian, much less the Pastor of a church! I figured he probably carried a switchblade where no one could see it and had a long criminal record... that's what Raider fans do, right? Now I'd learned my Pastor was a real football fan, and slightly crazy.

He kept surprising me year after year. One day he showed up around the church with a bandage on his face. I found out he had skin cancers that had to be removed surgically. I also found out he was allergic to all kinds of anesthesia. My dad told me he would just sit there and take it while they cut out the cancer on his face. ON HIS FACE! I learned my bald-headed Pastor was tough as nails.

Later I learned that he was really into guns and ammunition, that he liked to play golf, that people all over our state and even around the country respected him as a Bible scholar. I learned that he was a fine hunter and also a bit of a rebel.

I remember one year when our church was infested with pigeons. They were everywhere. Pastor hired my younger brother and I to get our BB guns and drive them off. I don't know how much good we did, but it sure was fun to play "Butch Cassidy and the Sundance Kid" under the full authority and permission of the guy who ran the church:

"What are you boys doing?"

"Shooting pigeons."

"Who said you could do that?"

"The Pastor!" And off we ran...

One of the greatest and most encouraging surprises came when I was in eighth grade. My Dad, the Youth Minister, had organized a door-to-door outreach on a Saturday morning. If you're unfamiliar with the terminology, this means you walk around the neighborhood and talk to people about Jesus, and try to help them see why it would be a great idea to give their lives to Him and come join us over at the First Baptist Church where we are learning to know Him better.

A couple of friends and I were working a particular street and we came to a particular house. When we knocked on the door a rather important looking man answered. We explained what we were doing and started talking about Jesus and what it means to know Him. We told him that he needed to give himself to Jesus if he wanted to have a worthwhile life and go to heaven. The man got sort of upset, and let us know that he was a member of First Baptist Church, knew the Pastor, and would be having a talk with him about our impertinent questions.

I didn't know what an impertinent was, but I thought I might be in a bit of trouble since I was acting as spokesman for the group. On the other hand, I thought, I had never seen this guy at church, so he was probably just blowing smoke to get us off his front porch. I'd probably never hear anything more about it.

Imagine my surprise a couple of weeks later when Dad walked in one evening and told me what had happened.

It seems my new friend *was* a member of our church, though he rarely showed up on a day that wasn't Christmas or Easter. It seems he *did* talk to the Pastor about my impertinent behavior. It also seems he was an important business owner in our town, and was used to getting what he wanted.

But not that day. He explained to the Pastor that I had been rude to him by telling him he should come to church, let Jesus run his life, and that this was the only hope he had. Pastor Misener just looked at him and nodded. He explained that everything I had said was true and right. He backed me up all the way.

I wasn't surprised that my Pastor would stand up for Jesus and the Bible. That's who he was, and what he did. But I was amazed that he would stand up for a kid like me. Without my knowing it, and for no other reason than integrity, he fought for me. He decided the skinny kid was worth too much to sacrifice to the important businessman. Surprised again.

After a while I guess I quit being surprised by Milford Misener. As the years went by I just started being encouraged and inspired by him. I found myself wanting to be like him in a variety of ways. His courage, his kindness, his integrity, his jump shot... and a whole lot more.

I watched him take care of his dying mother and show her the love and tenderness only a true son could give. I watched him suffer great losses and enjoy great victories with grace and courage. I've watched him be a true friend to my Dad for over 40 years; and I 'll tell you something – for a Raider fan, this guy is something else.

The books called First Samuel and Second Samuel in the Bible contain the story of David. David was a shepherd boy who became Israel's great King. I've mentioned him a time or two already, and he is certainly one of my favorites. At the moment, I am thinking about how surprising David tended to be.

The first time we meet David in the story he's a little brother. He is the youngest son of a sheep rancher named Jesse, and he gets all the rotten jobs. His older brothers have gone off to help King Saul fight Israel's enemies, and David has been left at home to shovel the sheep dip. This kid is boring.

As the story unfolds, however, we find out that David has actually fought and killed both a lion and a bear that attacked his father's sheep. A lion *and* a bear. With a slingshot. We also see David battle and defeat a giant that no other man in Israel has the courage to face.

Later David is chosen by God to be King of His people. He leads Israel to her greatest days. Along the way David writes some stellar music, excels as a military general, succeeds as an architect, and gains a reputation as "the man after God's own heart." I'm not saying the guy was successful or anything, but that star on Israel's flag just happens to be David's personal avatar.

The insignificant shepherd-boy becomes the Warrior King. And this should bother you. It should bother you because it violates everything your world has told you about significance.

In 1st Samuel Chapter 16, we read the story of the day God's prophet shows up at Jesse's house. Samuel knows that God has chosen one of Jesse's sons to be Israel's next king, but he doesn't know which son it is.

Samuel presumes the oldest and most impressive son will be the choice. The story says,

"When they arrived, Samuel saw Eliab and said, 'Certainly the Lord's anointed one is here before Him.' But the Lord said to Samuel, 'Do not look at his appearance or his stature, because I have rejected him. Man does not see what the Lord sees, man sees what is visible, but the Lord sees the heart.'" 1 Sam 16:6-7

Do you see it? More than meets the eye. One by one, each of the brothers is brought before the prophet; and one by one, they are passed over. Finally, Samuel looks around wondering if there are any more candidates. "Only little brother" comes the answer.

Samuel calls little brother in from the sheep pens, and God has His man. The rest, as they say, is history.

When an eleven-year-old boy who dreams of playing quarterback for the Denver Broncos meets a middle aged bald man who roots for the Oakland Raiders, the boy is likely to miss what's below the surface. He's likely to get wrapped up in what is visible.

But sometimes the boy is fortunate enough to be around long enough to see the skill, the toughness, the courage, and the faith. He gets to see the heart... and that changes the whole story.

8 AIM SMALL, MISS SMALL

Long after I had left home and started raising a family with my wife Kris, I saw a movie called *The Patriot*. Mel Gibson plays a reluctant Revolutionary War hero. Gibson's character finds himself in a fight for life and handing a black-powder musket to each of his two young sons. The boys will have to fire at Redcoat soldiers.

Gibson looks at his boys and asks, "What did I tell you fellows about shooting?"

The boys reply in unison. "Aim small, miss small."

Gibson repeats the phrase and nods in affirmation. "Aim small, miss small."

When I heard that line, I thought of Ted Peffer. He was a fine marksman and hunter, and he taught my brothers and me a great deal about how to shoot accurately.

Ted was already an old man when I met him. He was short

and skinny, with a bald head and a pair of glasses on his straight, thin nose. The dominant physical characteristics, though, were his hands and his feet. Ted Peffer had huge hands, and they were strong. I guess they served him well at work, because Ted was known as the best auto-glass man in town.

Oh yeah, the feet. I have no idea how big his feet were, I just knew that no one could keep up with him when it came time to walk. That old man could walk the legs off a tall horse, and he could go all day. Walking was sort of a contact sport for Ted… he took it seriously.

One day, not too long after we'd arrived in Belen, Ted called our house and told Dad he wanted to take the boys out to shoot some prairie dogs. We were thrilled. The words "out" and "shoot" always got our attention, and we liked Mr. Peffer, so life was good.

Pretty soon, Mr. Peffer pulled up in his old red pickup, and we piled in. I guess we drove for about a half hour, and entered a ranch on the west mesa above Belen. There, we learned the intricacies of shooting at prairie dogs. Ted explained that the ranchers hated prairie dogs – I believe the word vermin was used – because their towns caused all kinds of destruction on ranches, particularly when cattle or horses stepped in their holes and broke or sprained legs. For this reason, it was always open season on the little critters. The Brittain boys were more than happy to step in and rescue the herd.

Every warrior was given a .22 rifle and a box of shells. We would each get to shoot 25 times, keeping track of hits and misses. The shooter with the most kills would win the day.

I really don't remember how far we were from the targets. It seemed like a long way. I also don't recall how well we did, but I do know we improved in a hurry. Ted explained how we should set up, how we should squeeze the trigger, even how to breathe correctly. We had heard all of these things before, but this was a rare schoolhouse opportunity, and the Peffer Shooting Academy was in session.

We had no choice but to aim small, because prairie dogs are tiny. But Ted didn't want you to aim at the dog. He wanted you to aim at a spot on the dog. That's the key to aim small, miss small. If you're aiming at a spot and you miss it, you'll still probably hit the target. If you're aiming at a target and miss it, you'll probably get laughed at.

We learned that truth one day as we were leaving a dog-shoot. Ted had allowed us to ride in the back of the pickup, holding our rifles. He pulled up to talk to the ranch owner as we were heading out the gate. My brother looked over the side of the pickup bed and jumped back.

"There's a rattle snake down there!"

"Lemme see!"

Now there's one thing ranchers and cowboys and everyone else dislikes even more than prairie dogs, and that's rattle snakes. We knew our duty. We knew what we had to do. We were fortunately safe in the bed of Ted's pickup, about 10 feet from the snake. We looked him over for a minute, glanced at Ted and the rancher talking, and opened fire.

Aiming small sounds great until there's a live snake looking back at you. We couldn't hit him. Ted and the rancher looked around at us, and Ted got out of the pickup.

"What are you guys shooting at?" He asked.

My brother explained that there was a rattle snake over there.

"Did you kill it?"

"We missed, but we'll get him!"

Ted just reached up an empty hand, so I gave him my .22. He looked at the snake in a casual sort of way, pointed the rifle in a casual sort of way, and fired. Somehow, the snake's head sort of came apart. A .22 is plenty of firepower for a rattlesnake when you hit where you're aiming. Ted walked over and threw the dead snake into the brush and handed me my rifle. Another lesson learned.

A few months later, I was allowed to join the men on a quail hunt. I was excited and nervous because it would be my first try at quail hunting. We traveled south to the neighborhood of a mountain called *Ladrone*, which means "thief". It was where bandits used to hang out waiting to attack supply trains coming up the Rio Grande valley from Mexico. They would spot a train, then come screaming off the mountain to attack the merchants, steal their stuff, and take the ill-gotten gains back to the caves of Ladrone. At least that's how I heard the story. I guess people are still looking for outlaw treasure on that old mountain.

Mr. Peffer decided he would take me with him on the hunt. School was back in session. I carried a single-shot

.410, because my dad wasn't yet convinced that I was enough of a marksman to deserve the luxury of a second shot. Ted explained how quail behave, what to look for, and how to shoot them. I had good intentions, but I just couldn't stop aiming big.

The dog would jump a quail or two, I would swing my shotgun up, fire and miss, and Ted would shoot the quail. We had a great system working. As I recall, I finally hit one or two birds. I learned a lot that day, and I treasure the memory of my first hunt with Ted. Kid Paradise.

I really liked Ted Peffer. He was always patient, always ready to teach, and always ready to take care of whatever needed doing… he was a hard worker. He was consistent in his values and his behaviors, and because of this, the people in our church were always ready to listen to what he had to say. Ted lived an "aim small, miss small" kind of life.

He didn't aim small because he was afraid God would punish him if he missed. He aimed small because he knew God loved him. Like a bunch of the folks I knew at First Baptist Church in those days, Ted really believe that Jesus is *good*. He knew that he could only live a right life with God's help, and that it was worth the effort.

In the book of Romans, chapter 8, the Bible says, *Therefore, no condemnation now exists for those in Christ Jesus, because the Spirit's law of life in Christ Jesus has set you free from the law of sin and of death.* Rom 8:1-2

Here's the mystery. Some people approach Spiritual life as though God's plan is for them to get it done on their own.

They think God is always out to get you, and that you have to work hard to follow the rules so God won't strike you with lightning. They choose to live under the "law of sin and of death." They open fire on a prairie dog town with a sub-machine gun, and do more damage than the prairie dogs ever could.

Others decide that because of God's grace, they don't have to live any kind of life at all. They figure Jesus has "paid it all" and I can do whatever I want to. They become a law unto themselves and turn God's grace into something cheap and meaningless. They don't aim small. In fact, they really don't aim at all. They don't aim and they don't fire. They don't miss because there is no target. As far as they're concerned, the prairie dogs can have the whole ranch!

People like Ted are different, though. Ted had learned to aim small by living a long life of reliance on Jesus. He thought right, talked right, lived right and acted right because he had learned from the Master Marksman how to aim small. He obeyed the Savior because he really knew that was the best way to go. Ted believed the scripture that says,

For this is what love for God is: to keep His commands. Now His commands are not a burden, because whatever has been born of God conquers the world. This is the victory that has conquered the world, our faith. 1 John 5:3-4

The day Ted shot that rattlesnake, it didn't look to me liked he aimed at all. That was because he was so good at aiming that it came naturally. Shooting straight had become normal for him. It could have been a prairie dog or a quail or a charging elephant. It wasn't about the target, it was about the shooter.

That is just how he had come to live his life. He was free from the law because he was living to something greater. It wasn't about following rules or avoiding trouble. It was much more than that. Truly, the Spirit's law of life in Christ Jesus had set him free from the law of sin and of death. And that is a wonderful life to get to live.

9 BROTHERS

I grew up in an earthquake; or as some would call it, a house full of boys.

Living in a house full of boys means there's plenty of energy and creativity, and not nearly enough thinking about implications... which can lead to a whole lot of chaos. I still don't know how my Mother survived it. Makes you believe God really is powerful.

The three of us were evenly spaced and widely diverse. First came Mike, then two years –seven months later, I was born. Another two-and-a-half years brought my younger brother, David.

I mentioned that I've had stitches in my head a few times. Believe it or not, my brothers were present every time I cracked my head. The first time, it was completely their fault.

We got bored one night when I was about six and decided

to invent a game. The game was pretty simple, and a lot of fun. One brother would run across our room in the general direction of the bed, then jump as high as he could. Just as he jumped the other two – strategically positioned to the left and right of the path – would swing pillows at his legs. The result was a spectacular flip, a crash and riotous laughing.

The game was going along great until I made one particularly strong jump, and Mike and David make two particularly powerful swings. You see, there was this T.V. cabinet, and my head tried to share space with it... you get the picture.

My brothers and I were all different from the start. I mean different from each other, but some would say we were just plain different. We have different personalities, different talents, different senses of humor, and different football loyalties. Mike was always the best with guns and hunting, I was the best fisherman, and David was the best at stick-and ball sports.

Mike was always popular with the girls, David was popular with the guys, and I was popular with the parents... they knew if I was around their kids wouldn't get in trouble. Yeah, I was that guy. The rule follower. Mike was the rule breaker, and David was the little brother. Which means Mike and I usually thought the rules got changed to make his life easier.

I'm gonna pay for that one when he reads this. Did I mention he is the biggest? Yep, Dave's the biggest, and Mike's the toughest. But I'm the one you'd least want to fight. See, I've got these two brothers that are big enough and tough enough to whip anyone who messes with me.

Mealtime at our house was a lot like mealtime at an NFL training camp. Mom was a great cook, but when we were teenage boys, she probably could have put piles of salted cardboard on the table and we would never have known the difference. I'm still amazed at how much we could eat. The grocers in Belen used to send my Mom flowers at Christmas.

Then there were the smells. Sweaty football uniforms, dirty hunting clothes, various forms of decaying wildlife, fishy-smelling jeans (those were mine, the other guys' jeans just smelled like bait). There were greasy car smells, chemistry experiment smells, and more sweat. Then there were Mike's various bottles of cologne. He usually had a cloud of manly vapor floating above his head. Maybe that's why the girls liked him.

Mike was pretty good as big brothers go. He didn't ditch me very often, and he even let me tag along with his cool friends once in awhile. When I heard horror stories from my friends about their big brothers, I was thankful. Don't get me wrong, he did get frustrated with me a few times, and he did knock me around a little; but overall he treated me better than I deserved.

Some of my best memories with Mike involved birds and shotguns.

The nice thing about hunting birds is that it doesn't take much money and it doesn't take much time. We could walk a couple of hundred yards from the house and hunt doves or quail; and if we had a few hours, we'd go harass the ducks and geese.

Duck hunting with the Brittain boys was something you had to see to appreciate. You see, the Rio Grande runs right through the middle of Belen. It's a pretty big river when it has water in it.

Most of the water gets diverted for one reason or another, running down what we call irrigation ditches, on either side of the main channel. These irrigation ditches are really dirt canals that served to get water to where it is needed most. They may be a few feet from the river or a few miles, but they are the life-blood of the valley where we grew up.

Now the irrigations ditches have to be crossed all the time, so there are lots of bridges. The bridges were the first part of our hunting strategy. Recon. We'd crawl out onto a bridge with our binoculars, and look upstream and downstream. When we spotted some ducks, we'd mark their location with a nearby tree or some other landmark, and sneak off the bridge.

Now that recon was complete, it was time to advance the troops. Mike always took the lead, and bossed the operation. He was the oldest, and by far the most likely to hit something. The nice thing about those ditches was that they usually included a hill or road-bed running parallel to the water.

Sneaking upstream, behind the hill, we'd make our way to a spot just about even with where the ducks had been spotted. Mike would look at me and raise his eyebrows, and I'd nod. And then it happened.

Think of the Mel Gibson movie, *Braveheart.* Remember the scene where William Wallace led those crazy Scotsmen running into the teeth of the English lines? Yeah. We were like that. Two young warriors charging into battle. Those ducks had no chance. We'd come screaming over the top of the hill and the ducks would take off. Then we'd blast away with our twelve gauges. Sometimes we got a duck or two, and sometimes we didn't. But either way, we had a ball, and I'd love to do it again tomorrow.

One time in particular that sticks in my mind is the day my brother bagged that huge Canada goose. Neither of us had ever killed a goose, and we both wanted to. Goose hunting was hard. Geese are much more intelligent than Mallards, and hard to sneak up on. We didn't have decoys or any of that other fancy stuff... just our guns and our Mork.

"What's a Mork?" Great question. Mork was our black lab, and for my money, the best dog that ever lived. He was named after the Robin Williams character in the 70's sitcom *Mork and Mindy.* He retrieved every kind of bird you can shoot in New Mexico, and we loved him for it.

On this particular day, there was a stray goose hanging around the area we wanted to hunt. When we saw him, he became priority-one. The goose kept feeding in this low, wet area. Then he would lift off, circle around, and come back in.

Mike and I snuck around for a while and got in position. We hid the dog and ourselves, and waited – which is really the biggest part of hunting. During our wait, Mike sort of let me know it would be good for him to take a shot at that goose since he was the oldest, and the best shot, and had the keys...I figured he was right.

Pretty soon it happened. That old goose flew by and my big brother nailed him. Mork took off and brought the goose back just like the world-class dog he was. We had a grin-fest right there on the spot. Mork shivered with delight, nearly as proud as Mike was.

My brother was the hero of the day, and I was real happy for him. We took the goose back to his white Chevy pickup. I figured he'd want to get back home and show it off to Dad – which is what I would have wanted to do – so I started getting ready to go.

"Hey," says Mike. "Let's go get you a duck!"

And with that, we headed off into recon mode on the nearest bridge. Sure enough, there were a couple of mallards floating about 100 yards upstream. We sneaked up on them, stormed the hill, and I nailed the first green-head to clear the trees. Mork retrieved him like a champ. Kid Paradise.

When we got home, Dad took our picture with our trophy birds, and we begged Mom to cook them. She always hated cooking birds, probably because of the smell.

There were many hunts and sports and death defying games over the years, and many trips to the emergency room. There were a few fights, a bunch of campouts, and a host of weapons. There were dirt-bikes and summer jobs. There were first cars and first girlfriends. The three of us stormed our way through growing up with the subtlety and grace of a blind rhinoceros. But we all survived.

There were times – still are – when just for a moment, I'd like to lay a shovel alongside one of their heads. I expect my brothers have those moments, too, because we all sometimes forget what's true and act the fool. But those times don't tend to last, because we are brothers in more ways than one. We are brothers by DNA, and brothers in faith. We all belong to Jesus, and Jesus always comes after us. Jesus also whacks us on the side of the head when it's necessary. He has taught us how to handle those times like brothers.

Did you know two of Jesus' original disciples were brothers? Their names were James and John, and they were two of Jesus' closest friends. I think they may have been a little like my brothers and me, because of the nickname Jesus had for them. They were called, "The Sons of Thunder."

Sons of Thunder. "SOOOOOONNNS OOOOOOFF THUUUNNDERRRRRRR!" Can't you just hear it? Can't you just feel it? Can't you just smell it?

James and John were fishermen, and they worked for their Dad. The time they lived in, the job they worked, and the place they practiced their trade give you the idea that *Sons of Thunder* was a pretty right-on name for them.

The rest of Jesus' disciples were not much different. Peter and Andrew were also brothers, and worked with the Thunder boys on the lake of Galilee. The rest of them, as far as we know, were also working-class guys. One was a revolutionary, and one was a liar. Every group needs a nerd to pick on, and that was Matthew. He was a tax agent.

As best we can tell, the twelve were fairly young, fairly uneducated, and completely male. Which leads me to the view that these guys were a whole lot more like the Brittain boys than most of the folks at the church think they were.

I see Jesus and the boys sitting around the campfire at night, roasting *Hebrew National* hot dogs, making s'mores and laughing at each other. I see wrestling matches and fishing contests, and probably some things that would draw a "That's disgusting!" from a woman.

One time, James and John got their Mom to approach Jesus and ask Him if her boys could be the top dogs in His new Kingdom. The other guys got hot in a hurry. I think there might have been a beatdown if Jesus hadn't intervened.

I guess what I'm trying to say is that, like my brothers and me, Jesus' disciples were a bunch of small-town dudes. And like us, they had their great moments and their not-so-great moments.

After Jesus died, the disciples sort of scattered for a bit. When they came back together, they didn't know what to do with themselves. Peter, who was the leader in many ways – and also the most likely to say the wrong thing - decided to go fishing. The rest of the guys went with him. This story is recorded in John Chapter 21, and it is one of my favorites.

While the guys were fishing, Jesus showed up on the shore, incognito. He hooked them up with a miraculous catch of fish, and called them over. They started toward the stranger on the shore, and soon realized who it was. The boys got excited, and Peter the Brave launched himself into the waist-deep water and swim-walked to shore. The rest of the guys brought the boat in, cooked some fish and had breakfast.

After the meal, Jesus took Peter aside. This had to be a rough moment for old Pete. He knew that just a few days before, he had bragged to Jesus about how faithful he would be... how he would stick no matter what the rest of these losers did.

Within a few hours of that conversation, Peter denied even knowing Jesus, cussed at some people, and walked away in shame. Now Jesus was taking him aside. Ouch.

What Jesus did next is legendary, and a critical lesson for every dude out there. He looked Peter in the eye – man to man – and invited him back into the hunt. He reminded Peter of what was true, and promised him that for the rest of Peter's life, and even in his death, he would be on Jesus' team.

In the days that followed, Peter became the leader of the world-changing movement called the Church. Peter came back from the edge of destruction, and became just the man Jesus made him to be. Amazing.

Peter, Andrew, James, John. Michael, Ricky, David. Dudes from a small town whose lives were changed by a man named Jesus. Men Jesus keeps inviting, and always will. Brothers who learned from the Master what it means to be a man.

Wanna wrestle?

10 FULL THROTTLE

The green ten-speed wasn't my favorite bike in Belen. My favorite bike was a Suzuki. It was blue, it was cool, and it had a motor. One-hundred twenty-five ccs of raw power... which may not sound like much, but was plenty for a skinny kid who never had quite enough love for the brakes.

My dirt bike was one of the best ways I ever found to have a great time and sacrifice skin. I can't remember how many times I wrecked it, but there were some spectacular spills.

We lived in a dirt-bike Mecca, high on the western slope of the Rio Grande Valley. Our house sat just a half-mile from the true rise of the west mesa (Spanish word – means table – and refers to a flat-topped hill or mountain). The mesa was made primarily of dirt, and was an endless network of trails. You could ride all afternoon and never cover the same spot twice. There were tough hills and jumps, sudden drop-offs, and lots of arroyos you could fall into. Flash floods were always reshaping the terrain, so you had to stay alert if you didn't want to break your bike or your body.

Many afternoons, when I got home from school, I'd throw on my helmet and head west to burn up a few trails before dinner. These were great times, but even better were the night rides.

Don't tell my Mother about this, but a couple of friends and I used to go out at night and chase jackrabbits by the light of the moon.

Now I know what you're thinking. "What kind of fool would chase a jackrabbit in the dark on a motorcycle. It's clear you're not going to catch one, and what would you do with it if you did?"

Good question. I firmly believe that only car-chasing dogs and teenage boys can understand why this is a good idea. Since I am not a dog, and no longer a teenage boy, I can't help you with the answer. But I do remember that it was an absolute blast.

Now that I'm more mature, I would never encourage anyone to take this up as a hobby, and I readily admit it was a poor decision.

For one thing, not all of us had headlights, and even the light of a *full* moon is sketchy at best. Furthermore, chasing a jackrabbit at 35 miles an hour in the dark poses some real problems. Jackrabbits can turn much more quickly and sharply than motorcycles... which leads to the sacrifice of some large patches of skin.

The biggest problem, though, was that you couldn't always see where you were headed. Some genius had left quite a few logs and boulders lying around, and then there was the ditch.

An irrigation ditch ran along the east edge of our favorite rabbit-chasing range. As I've mentioned, the ditches were sometimes dry and sometimes filled with water. One night I was particularly focused on a particular jackrabbit. Hot pursuit.

As seems to have been the case many times in my teenage years, *several things happened at once*: I notice a significant rise in the ground, the jackrabbit darted to the left, and I spied the vague outline of trees in front of me.

The only trees anywhere around were on *the other side of the ditch*. Just as I decided it would be a good idea to slam on the brakes and lay the bike down, I went airborne.

I'd love to say I soared over the ditch, executed a perfect Evel Knivel landing, and turned around to salute my buddies. The reality was less impressive and more painful. Airborne might have been too strong a word. I did hit a rise, and I did leave the ground, but there was nothing that could have been mistaken for flying. I just sort of tumbled into the ditch.

Oh, I know what you're thinking. I know what you want to ask me....

"Was there water in the ditch?"

Well, let me ask you a question. "What would you prefer?" You see, water is softer than dirt and rocks, and my landing would probably have been less painful in water. On the other hand, because there was no water, my bike didn't float away to oblivion; which is why my Father allowed me to live.

There was no water, and my landing was anything but soft. I flew off the bike and landed in a heap next to it. After taking a few moments to make sure I wasn't dead, I got busy trying to drag the bike out of the ditch. I still cannot remember how we got it done. I think that was my last night ride.

The very best times on the dirt bikes were the times I rode with Dad. He had an awesome bike, a Suzuki PE 250. It was a monster, and I think it could have climbed the side of a glass skyscraper. What a machine.

I was scared of it. Well, I was scared of it at first. But you know the drill. After a while, I got better and gained confidence. Then I began to look at the PE with longing. I wanted to ride it. I could handle it.

I began to pester my Dad about the big Suzuki, and finally, he decided I could give it a go. After tooling around a bit, I felt it was time to try something that could cost me some skin. How about a jump?

"Okay, Ricky. See that little bump over there? Just ride across the open and go over that. But keep your speed down!"

"Yes, sir."

"You hear me? Keep your speed down. That's a powerful bike!"

"Ok."

I rode a couple hundred yards in the opposite direction and swung around. I approached my target jump cautiously, keeping the speed down. As I got closer, I somehow convinced myself that this machine wasn't as powerful as I had thought. If I was going to get any air at all, I needed some *speed*. I didn't want to just roll over it, I wanted to get airborne! I gunned it.

My Dad stepped it off later and said I flew at least twenty-five feet – which is really something considering the tiny hill I used for a launching pad. As I flew over the handle bars, I thought, "this is gonna hurt." It did.

That was the day I made my greatest contribution to the skin-gods. I sort of scraped off the left side of my chest. Kid paradise? Maybe...

After that, I spent some more time on the 250 and got where I could handle it better. This was good, because I still had one serious challenge to overcome.

On the west mesa, above Belen, there's a particularly steep hill – sort of a butte – with a giant white letter "B" emblazoned on its face. The B looks down on the high school football field and inspires the Eagles to victory. It also inspires young men on motorcycles to death-defying feats.

The B was sort of the holy grail of trails for us. It took a bike with lots of power to climb that hill. The narrow trail between the white letter B and the edge of the hill-face meant it also took a rider with courage. And I really wanted to climb it. I had tried many times on my little 125 enduro, and I just couldn't make it. Not enough power.

The only way I was going to go over the top of the B was on the big bike. One summer evening, Dad finally gave me permission to try it.

We set up way back from the base of the hill, and he gave me some advice. "Keep your eyes up – look where you're going, and avoid that big boulder on the right. If you get in trouble, lay it down and keep clear of the bike. And no matter what you do, *keep your speed up*."

Wait, did he say, "keep your speed up?" This guy has never told me to keep my speed up on a motorcycle. He's always telling me to be safe or smart or some other boring thing. What gives?

I stared back at Dad, and he read my mind. "I know, but if you don't keep your speed up, you'll never get to the top."

It took a few tries before I learned to keep my speed up like I needed to, but I'm happy to report that finally, that beautiful machine screamed its way straight to the top. As I sat high atop the B, looking down on the cars zipping by on Interstate 25, I felt as alive as I'd ever felt. It had been a thrill, and an accomplishment. I was on top of the world. Kid paradise.

The reality of climbing a hill like that one is that you *do* have to keep your speed up or you won't make it. When a biker approaches a rough, steep hill, he's counting on that machine to carry him to the top, and the machine has to have fuel to operate.

Many people approach life and faith with lots of caution, and not much fuel. They take it easy. They go slow because they don't want to get hurt. They mis-use phrases like "wait on the Lord" to justify their cautious approach to life with God. But when you look at the scriptures that tell us to wait on the Lord, you find an interesting reality.

These scriptures talk about waiting on God to restore your strength, or to rescue you, or to return for His church. The waiting is about being patient as you look to God to *come through* for you. The scriptures about waiting on the Lord are never about waiting to do what God has told you to do!

The scriptures are packed full of instructions from God. These instructions are for our good, and they are for God's glory. They are not suggestions or nice ideas. They are the way our creator has instructed us to live, and they work. They work best when we "go all in" as the poker players say.

There's a story in the Bible about a guy who had to learn to open the throttle. In the book of Judges, Chapters 6-8, we read about Gideon. Gideon was the son of a farmer, and God called him out to rescue the people of Israel from the oppression of some foreign kings.

At the beginning of the story, God sends his angel to call Gideon out, and his greeting is epic. *"The Lord is with you, mighty warrior!"* Now that's a greeting. I'd love to tell you that Gideon responds with powerful faith, and steps up right away. But he doesn't.

Gideon keeps asking God to give him signs, just to make sure he is hearing God right. He puts some sheep hair – called fleece – on the ground and asks God to make dew fall on the fleece, but not the ground around it. Then Gideon reverses the request, asking God to wet the ground, but not the fleece. After God patiently grants these two requests, Gideon becomes convinced, and opens the throttle.

The next section of the story tells about Gideon becoming a mighty warrior and a mighty leader. He leads Israel to defeat their enemies by God's power. He shares the glory of God's victory with others, and he leads the people of Israel to freedom. At the end of the story, everyone wants to make Gideon their king, but he turns them down. "I will not rule over you, and my son will not rule over you; the Lord will rule over you."

This is a beautiful picture of a man who trusts God and acts on the instructions he's been given. Gideon has learned that once the Lord speaks, it is no longer time to wait on Him. Gideon is like a powerful dirt bike screaming up a mighty hill. The throttle is wide open and the power is flowing.

When a follower of Jesus trusts his master enough to open the throttle of obedient faith, the power surges. Just like gasoline flooding into the carburetor, the Spirit of God fills and empowers the disciple, and several things happen.

God's plans get carried out in his life.

He gets to know God better and take on more of His character.

Other people Jesus loves get set free, too.

There's nothing better than running free on a mission from God. It is where we were designed to live, and it is where we are at our best. Like Dad said, "If you don't keep your speed up, you'll never get to the top."

So ponder this, Mighty Warrior:

The Lord is with you. Do you trust God enough to open the throttle?

11 FAITHFUL LOVE

As I've mentioned, our home was all-energy all the time.
My Dad, my brothers and I were forever building
something or destroying something; experimenting and
inventing; making messes, demanding food and bulldozing
our way through life. I feel tired just thinking about it.
Those were chaotic days, and they were great days. I miss
them.

In the midst of the chaos and the feeding frenzies, there
lived a woman. She was a beautiful lady with brown hair
and brown eyes. She had a birthmark high on her right
cheek, and the slightest Oklahoma accent, that came out
more strongly when she got around her relatives. She was
all the things nostalgic men tend to remember about their
mothers…whether they are true or not. Make no mistake.
In our case, they are true.

She was soft-spoken, patient, gentle and loving.
She was a great cook and a brilliant seamstress, and she
was loving.
She was a wonderful story-teller, a creative designer, and
very loving.

My Mother's love bubbled to the surface in a million different ways. Sometimes it was sudden and spectacular, like an unexpected birthday cake. More often, it was clothed in the mundane... cooking and cleaning and bandaging and fixing. Sometimes it was a lesson captured in just the right moment. That's what happened the day my brother started a fight with me.

David might tell you it was me who started it, but we both know better. I don't recall whether it began outside or inside, and I certainly don't remember what it was about. Whatever the reason, it was the classic story... the foolishness of youth.

We had been told many times not to argue and fight. We knew the rule, but like so many boys, we didn't really grasp its meaning. All David and I knew was that we each wanted to be right and get our way. I know you've never experienced this yourself, dear reader, but some of us struggle. We were tossing shouts and insults back and forth like a football, and the anger was escalating quickly.

Our fight was going along quite nicely until Mom showed up. You'd be amazed at how quickly a single word from her could change the course of our behavior. I'd love to say it was because of our deep love and respect for her, but it was mostly because she had the hotline to Dad, and we knew Dad liked her more than he liked us. If we didn't show respect to Mom, we might find ourselves living on the mean streets of small-town New Mexico.

"Boys!" Was all she had to say.

We stopped in our tracks, staring daggers at one another.

What followed was one of those pointless conversations parents start with angry kids: What's going on? What happened? Why can't you treat each other like you should?

I'd like to say I stood up for my little brother and took the blame, but that would be somewhere far from the truth. I threw him under the bus. But don't worry, he wasn't alone down there. He did a little under-bussing of his own.

Mom finally stopped asking questions and told us to go to our rooms. This is the point in the movie where the hero screams "Noooooooooo!" as the enemy mortar shell hits his foxhole. "Go to your room" meant, "I'm going to let your Dad handle this." David and I both knew what was coming next. We would have to deal with Dad, and that probably meant a spanking. Nowhere close to Kid Paradise.

Please understand. I'm not complaining. I'm not claiming abuse. I deserved many more spankings than I ever got, and looking back now, I am truly thankful for every one of them. I firmly believe every spanking was an act of love, and they probably kept me from ruining my own life. My parents knew what they were doing. Those few spankings were a low price to pay for learning right from wrong.

I believe in spankings, but they still hurt, and I didn't want one. Oh well. Some days are diamonds and some days are leather...

We each sat in a quiet room, pondering our own mortality. Then we heard a voice. "Boys, come here."

It wasn't the voice we expected. It was Mom. We emerged from our rooms like a couple of rabbits wondering if the coyote is still around. Was this a trick? Had Mom grown so weary of our arguing that they had decided to ambush us? Mom told us to sit on the couch. She stood in front of the two offenders like a reluctant judge. Then she spoke.

"Boys, today we're going to learn about grace."

We stared back. Puzzled both by her words and by the lack of action. "Grace? Is this some new kind of punishment? What do you mean, grace?"

I'd certainly heard about grace before that. You have to remember, I'd been going to church exactly nine months longer than I had been breathing on my own. I knew all the words to *Amazing Grace*, and all the Bible stories that those words came from. I was confused. Mom continued to speak.

"We're going to keep this between us," she said. "I won't tell your Dad about it."

Mom went on to explain to us about exactly what God's love means, and what grace cost Him. She said she was going to show us that kind of love, and never mention the fight again.

We were stunned. Guilty as sin, and caught red-handed, we'd been given a pardon. Because we had messed up before and been punished, we knew exactly what we were being given. This grace was a treasure, kind of like the grace God still offers us. Amazing grace! How sweet it sounded. And yes, we felt like a couple of wretches who had been saved.

Angels began to sing. Victory trumpets sounded. There was a glowing light around my sainted Mother's face. Our tears of anger and fear became tears of joy. To this day, David is convinced that it was in that moment that God really called both of us to become Pastors.

I am confident that she told Dad every bit of it. She probably explained that she had taken the opportunity to teach us about grace and that he needed to keep his mouth shut. They probably prayed that God would use this to teach us a lesson so no one would have to listen to our arguing any more. Parents are sneaky like that. I can attest that neither of my parents ever spoke of it, and that my Mom promises she has no recollection of the events of that day.

My little brother is now a smart guy. He has a Doctorate and can read the Bible in Hebrew. He was talking the other day about a Hebrew word: Hesed. For your enjoyment, the H has to have a lot of spit in it, and the emphasis is on the first syllable. Try it, 'Cchhhe-sed'. Not bad. Try again, but with more spit.

My smart brother says this little word in Hebrew can't really be translated to English, and that it takes a pretty long paragraph in English to describe it well. Hesed is the "faithful love" that God showed to Israel and shows to us. It is a love that puts the other person first. It is relentless and unending. Hesed is described in Philippians chapter two with these words:

"Do nothing out of rivalry or conceit, but in humility consider others
as more important than yourselves. Everyone should look out not only
for his own interests, but also for the interests of others.
Make your own attitude that of Christ Jesus,
who, existing in the form of God,
did not consider equality with God
as something to be used for His own advantage
Instead He emptied Himself
by assuming the form of a slave,
taking on the likeness of men.
And when He had come as a man
in His external form,
He humbled Himself by becoming obedient
to the point of death—
even to death on a cross. Phil 2:3-8

You see, the ultimate expression of Hesed was the birth,
life and death of Jesus. God literally made Himself
nothing. He put us first. He set aside his rights and set up
His tent in our camp. All the dirt and noise and
foolishness that was human life on earth, Jesus chose to
voluntarily enter into.

It was this entering in that allowed Jesus to show us the
truth about love. Which brings me back to Mom. She set
aside her rights and set up her tent in what would become
our camp. She took on all the dirt and noise and
foolishness.

I fear that many people never experience that kind of love. God offers it, but they never learn to receive. Many more live desperate lives, surrounded by crowds of people who don't offer any love, much less selfless, faithful love. I, on the other hand, had Hesed pouring my Cheerios every morning.

My mother lived love every time she rushed me to the emergency room. She lived selflessness when she insisted she wasn't hungry and gave extra to one of us who always was. She lived Hesed as we walked together on the journey of learning to live with my diabetes. She even helped me pick out the engagement ring I would offer to the woman who would take her place in so many ways.

Now, she teaches this way of living to her grandchildren as she and Dad pray for them and support their dreams and the journey God has plotted for each of them. I watch my children experience faithful love, and I watch them want to join in.

This kind of faithful love is startling to our world. People don't know what to do with it. Sometimes they simply reject. Sometimes they work up the courage to trust it. Most often, I think, they just can't believe it is possible. But I know better.

Faithful love has brown hair and brown eyes, and a birthmark high on her right cheek.

12 LORD AND MASTER

It was an early morning in early December. The ground was frosty, and the air was, too. The sun peeked over the rim of the Manzano Mountains, just a few miles to the east. My brother walked just a few feet to my right. The sky was crystal blue, and steam rose from the water. All these things were true, and they were worth noting, but I didn't note them. I only had eyes for Mork.

The beautiful, smart, full of life and love black Labrador retriever worked just a few paces in front of us. He cast back and forth looking, smelling, seeking. I followed Mork through the brush and trees, every sense alert. My hand rested on the trigger guard of the twelve-gauge Remington. Then the silence was broken as *several things happened all at once*:

As Mork's head shot up and he froze in place, there was an explosion of flapping wings. A wave of pure energy and a moment of terror swept over me as the cock pheasant shot from the brush. I caught my breath, gathered myself and threw the Remington to my shoulder. Just like I had been taught, I swung the muzzle left to right, pointing at the big pheasant. As I passed his flight path, I squeezed the trigger, and – to my delight and surprise – the pheasant tumbled to the earth.

"Bird, Mork!" I yelled, grinning all the while. Mork was off like a shot, quickly proving that his breed was rightly named. The muscle rolled beneath his ebony coat. It was poetry in motion. He brought the bird to me, carrying it gently in his mouth. I swear that dog could retrieve a bird without ruffling a single feather.

"Give." I said, reaching down.

He dropped the pheasant in my hand and smiled up at me as if to say, "Nice shot, kid. You're getting the hang of this." What a dog.

Not all days were as perfect as that one. One time, I had girl trouble.

It was the usual kind of girl trouble. The kind where you like a girl and think she likes you, then find out different. I went to the back yard and sat down with my back to the house. I wanted to think and mope, maybe shed a tear. I was gearing up for a full-on pity party. Mork ambled over with a stick in his mouth.

"Here's an idea," he said. "You throw this stick way over there by the fence, and I'll run over and bring it back." Well, he didn't say it, but it was pretty clear what he had in mind.

"Get lost," I responded. "Can't you see I'm trying to be

miserable here?"

"Awe, c'mon, kid. Throw the stick. Just once. I guarantee it'll make you feel better." Then he dropped it in my lap.

"Fine." I picked up the stick and threw it way over by the back fence. Mork was off like a shot again. (He was off like a shot pretty often, now that I think about it.) The stick was back in about five seconds, laying in my lap.

I threw again. Now the problem with Mork was that once you threw the stick twice, you were sort of committed, and he knew it. The second retrieve was much more exciting than the first, because he knew the game was on.

I started trying to outsmart Mork by throwing the stick in hard-to-reach places or making fake throws. It was like trying to cheat at chess against Bobby Fisher - no chance. After a couple dozen throws, I sort of forgot about my girl trouble and got happy about life again. Leave it to Mork to remind me what's not important.

It wasn't just sticks with that dog. He had a thing for logs, too. Once in a while, he'd make his way over to the woodpile and choose a log. The perfect log would range from about a foot to a foot-and-a-half long and was around four inches thick.

The chosen log would become an important part of Mork's life. He would carry it around with him and chew on it. A lot of dogs carry a chew toy, but most of those don't weigh five or ten pounds. It was like his work-out regimen; as though he knew it was his job to protect our home against enemy invasion, and he had to be in top shape at all times.

A log would last Mork a few weeks. After he'd chewed his way through it, the two half-logs would be cast aside and he'd claim a new one. I remember walking out the back door of the house and calling that dog, then seeing him stop to pick up the log before he came to me.

I don't know why the logs were so important to Mork, but they were. And that's the striking thing about a dog like him. Lots of people think dogs lack focus; that all you have to do to distract them is yell "Squirrel!" and they'll be off on a new chase after nothing.

Lots of dogs (and lots of people) lack focus. They're easily distracted. The beauty about Mork is that he was driven by the things that were important to him, which was visible in how he went about his business. What made Mork a great hunting dog was his ability to focus. I've seen a rabbit run by while he was hunting birds and draw nothing more than a sidelong glance. When it was time to find a down bird, he would absolutely not be distracted, and he would never give up.

When he rode in the back of our pickup, you could park and leave him there with two great certainties: Mork would not leave the truck under any circumstances, and no one would lay a hand on our vehicle or anything in it.

Mork would worry over his log like it meant everything to him, and he always stuck with it 'til the log was chewed through, and the job was done. Only then would he pick a new one.

But of all the important things in Mork's life, nothing came before his masters. My Dad, my brothers and I, even Mom could gain his full attention simply by walking through the door into our backyard. Only we could distract Mork from his log; only we could assure him that a stranger was welcome; and only we could convince him to ignore the birds. Mork's single-minded focus could be instantly and completely shifted by one word from his Lords.

Lord. Does that word bug you? It bothers lots of people. We don't appreciate terms like Lord, because they indicate someone else is in charge; or worse yet, in charge of me. Many people just can't understand why you would want to call someone else Lord. I think Mork can teach us a great deal on the subject.

One of the Greek words translated "worship" in the New Testament of the Bible finds it's meaning in dogs like Mork. It means, "to kiss, like a dog licking his master's hand." It is a picture of complete love and subjection to someone else. This is what Mork practiced in his life with us. Because of this practice, his life was the best it could be.

Mork was a retriever. It was built into his nature. But he couldn't retrieve without one of us to throw the stick or shoot the bird.

He was a joyful dog – he loved to jump and run and to celebrate. We gave him something to celebrate.

He was a brave protector, and we gave him a home and a family to protect.

Can a dog love? I don't know – I'm not a dog. But I do know that my family and I were the beneficiaries of Mork's devotion, and the center of his attention. I can't help think that Mork's limited ability to understand love and devotion, compared to ours, is a lot like our limited ability compared to God's.

Mork knew whatever form of love he might have known because of us. He had purpose in his life because of us. He was cared for and loved by us. What dog wouldn't want to declare Lordship for the humans who gave him all that?

This kind of worship is great because it's a two-way street. While my family and I gave Mork a great deal, he gave us a lot, too. He gave us lots of joy. We delighted in him just like the Savior delights in His children.

And that's how it is with Jesus and me. Without Him, there's no purpose. Without Him, there's no joy. Without Him, there's no hope. Without Him, there's no love. But with Jesus, there is all of this – and more.

Something to believe in.

Someone to belong to.

Something to live for.

And who wouldn't want a Lord like that?

13 THE GIFT

There's an old proverb that says, "Give a man a fish and feed him for a day. Teach a man to fish and feed him for a lifetime."

The more accurate version of this quote would be, "Give a man a fish and feed him for a day. Teach a man to fish and watch him starve to death!"

Like a lot of hobbies guys pick, fishing can be frustrating. Not as frustrating as golf, but frustrating nonetheless. Since I've spent my whole life fishing, I've seen, and experienced, plenty of frustration.

Other people see fishing as a hobby, or a vocation, or a stress reliever. Fishing can be a passion, and it can be a romance. It is certainly a quest, and a never-ending adventure. Oh, and did I mention frustrating?

But for me, while fishing is all of those things, it is first something else. Fishing is a gift.

Not an "ability" kind of gift, though I am pretty stinkin' good at it. Fishing is a gift that is bestowed... a given gift.

The first one I remember giving me the gift was my Father's Father. Papa was known far and wide as a first-class trout fisherman. Papa had a boat and he had a lake. He didn't own the lake, but Bluewater was – no doubt – my Papa's lake. He knew every inch of it. He knew when and where the fish would be biting, and what bait to use.

And he had a boat! When I was a kid, on days we couldn't go fishing, I would wash the boat just to be close to it. I remember sitting in Papa's boat with my Zebco 202 clutched in my little fist, just waiting for a trout to bite. You guessed it – Kid Paradise!

I guess Papa's gift to me could be called the love of fishing. Papa was a fisherman, and because of him, and what he shared with me, I wanted to be a fisherman, too. When we were out on the boat or on the shore of Bluewater lake, life felt perfect. We could have been a lot of places, doing a lot of different things. Lots of people would have chosen something else... but not us. We loved fishing. I don't know why, we just did.

If I'm honest, I know there are things Papa taught me that were more important than to love fishing: his love for Jesus and the people in his community, his high regard for God's word, and the ability to stand in front of a bunch of people and preach the gospel of Jesus are a few. But I sure am glad he took us fishing when we were little. He gave me a treasure then that we shared for the rest of his life, and he bestowed one of the great loves of my life. What a gift.

If Papa gave me the love for fishing, there's no doubt that his son – my Dad – gave me the science. Dad taught me how to fish. He taught me how to cast every kind of rod, what kind of baits and hooks to use for every kind of fish. He taught me beautiful words like Mepps, twenty-pound test, treble hook and open-faced reel.

My Dad taught me how to tie a necktie, a half-hitch and a saddle-girth, but there's no doubt that the *improved clinch knot* is the most important knot he ever blessed me with. By the way, if you don't know what an improved clinch knot is, I'll make you a deal… you don't tell anybody, and I won't either.

There are a lot of kids who want to go fishing. My personal belief is that every kid wants to go fishing, whether they know it or not. I was fortunate and happy because my Dad *took* me fishing. We logged a lot of hours, and had a lot of adventures framed around fishing, and by the time I was in junior high school, I could handle myself around water pretty well. Dad and I have fished together many more times since then – everything from white bass at Elephant Butte to sea trout on the Inter-coastal Waterway to wild Alaskan salmon on the Kenai River. Good times. The best of times.

All of which brings me to the third gift. If my Papa gave me the love and my Dad gave me the science, I'd have to say the art came from a guy named Oscar Cole. Now if you know Oscar, you may have just laughed out loud, because Oscar is not what you'd call an artsy guy.

Oscar used to be a high-school history teacher in Belen, and a lover of all things outdoors. Besides history, he taught a lot of kids to play baseball and basketball and a bunch of other things. But he taught me something else.

Oscar taught me how to fish with a fly rod.

Did you ever watch *A River Runs Through It?* Fly-fishing is what the guys in that movie do. It involves creating an artificial model of a bug, tying it on the end of a line, and delivering it in such a way that a fish – a trout in particular – will choose to eat it. The glorious result of this transaction is that a six-foot man with a college education, having invested all kinds of money, time and effort, will succeed in outsmarting a creature with a brain the size of a BB, only to set it free within seconds of capture. The six-foot man will then feel that his life has meaning and that he can go back down to the valley and take on the world. Or something like that.

It was the summer after my sophomore year of high school that I was invited by three of the men in our church to go on a fishing trip. We had our sights set on a big fish-fry for the families, and the thing we needed most was some fresh trout for the main course. I don't know that we ever had that fish-fry. I think it was just an excuse to go.

In those days, the legal limit for trout in New Mexico was 8 per day, 16 in possession. Our plan was to drive down to Snow Lake in the Gila Wilderness (the G sounds like an H) of Southwestern New Mexico, spend a couple of days, and come home with 64 trout. Perfect.

John Lucero lived across the street from us, so we got our gear together and met Oscar over at Ron Cooke's house. We threw all our stuff in Ron's camper and hit the road early in the afternoon. The last half of the drive to Snow Lake is dusty and bumpy... kinda like the last half of the drive to nearly every worthwhile fishing spot in New Mexico. The dust and bumps are immediately washed away in the cool mountain air and ponderosa pines that surround the small reservoir on the middle fork of the Gila River.

We got to the lake and set up camp, then made some dinner and settled in to watch the sun go down. The next morning, we got up and hit the lake.

Remember how frustrating fishing can be? This was one of those days. We fished all morning and none of us got a bite, which was both shocking and troubling considering the high quality of fisherman we're talking about here. A game warden came by and explained that due to heavy rains, the lake had turned over. Water was pouring out the spillway, and the fish simply weren't biting. No one had caught anything on that lake all week.

John and I decided to take a walk, so we went over the top of the dam and down the middle fork. The stream was running high and muddy, but I kept glancing over at it. It was water we hadn't fished yet, I had a rod and bait, and... I finally gave in.

"Hey John, let's wet a hook."

"Here? This water is high and muddy and ... O.K."

I put on a salmon egg with a small split-shot weight and dropped my hook in the creek. In less time than it takes for the first fisherman to start lying, I had one on. We caught a couple more, and headed back to let the guys know how brilliant we were, and invite them to share the fruits of our greatness.

I'm almost ashamed to say it, but we snuck back to camp. It's true. We didn't want anyone messing up our fishing spot, so we climbed up a ridge and made our way around the bottom end of the lake, dropping onto the trail far from our secret honey-hole.

You should have seen the heads turn as we walked along the trail with fish on a stringer. I was smug, but cool. Everyone asked where we had caught them, and we happily shared the knowledge.

Okay, we didn't share a thing. We employed the fisherman's vague wave. "Over toward the dam. Not much, but at least we didn't get skunked." Our humility was particularly striking, since we were the only two people to have seen a live fish anywhere near that lake in almost a week.

"What were you using?" the poor fishless creatures asked.

"Salmon eggs." And with the superior air only a successful fisherman can muster, we strutted up the path.

We ate a late lunch, and before long the four of us were back on the creek getting a bite on every cast. Though we only kept the best fish, we had our limit in a couple of hours, and snuck back to camp. We cleaned the fish, put them on ice and settled back to ponder our victory.

The next day, we returned to the creek to haul in another limit. As we fished, I noticed Oscar was using a strange rod. He would fling it back and forth, a growing length of heavy lined extending from the top of the rod, then he'd let it fall on the creek and the water would explode as a fish grabbed the bait.

That looked fun. I watched for a while and decided it looked like a *lot* of fun. The rod was longer than our spinning rigs, and it would bend deeply as he played the trout - real fishing magazine stuff.

"Hey Oscar. What's that?"

"Huh?" Oscar was always big on that word. He was a "Huh" kind of guy.

"What's that rod?" I asked again.

"Oh. It's a fly rod. You put a bug on the end of it and use the weight of the line to get it out there."

"Cool! Can I try it?"

"Nah. You'd just get yourself tangled up in it." Oscar and I were never afraid to give each other a little grief.

"Ok, old man. Don't hurt yourself." I went back to fishing. Since I'd been the one to discover this hole, and none of them would have caught a single fish without me, I didn't feel the need to humble myself any further.

But I couldn't get that image out of my mind. I wanted to fish like that. A fly rod. Interesting.

As soon as I got home, I started pestering Oscar to teach me to fly-fish. I went to T-G and Y - the closest thing Belen had to a sporting-goods store in those days – and bought myself a kit: fly rod, reel and line for only 24.99. It even had an auto-retrieve reel, which I assumed meant it was a superior model.

Oscar showed me how to put everything together, assured me that I'd be throwing that auto-retrieve reel in the trash by Christmas, and we made plans to head to the Jemez (J=H) mountains.

Oscar took me to a small stream called the *Rio De Las Vacas* – "River of the Cows" for you English speakers – and we set up camp under a big old cottonwood tree right by the water.

My tutor explained to me that there are two kinds of flies – dry and wet – and that we would be using dry flies, which float on top of the water, and imitate mature insects riding on the surface. We did a little work on entomology (the study of bugs), and he continued the casting lessons that had begun a couple of weeks before.

Oscar strolled over to the river and said, "Stand next to me, always on my left, or you'll get a hook through your ear." Got it. Standing to the left.

"See that tree hanging over the bank? See the shade? How the current comes around that rock? There's a fish right there and I'm gonna catch it."

"Oh you are, are you?" This was too much. I knew Oscar Cole. He was a big jokester... thought he was funny. Come to think of it, he still thinks he's funny. I figured Oscar was just yanking my chain like he did all the time. I decided to let him hang himself in his own rope, and settled back to watch Oscar do his thing. I figured he'd end up with his fly caught in that tree, and fall down in the river as a bonus.

He looked behind him, shook out a little line and started casting. The fly whizzed back and forth a few times as the line shot out. Then he let it settle on the water just to the left and above the rock he'd pointed out. As I watched the fly drift downstream, there was an explosion. Oscar set the hook, and before I could figure out what was happening, he had a brown trout in his net.

I was dumbfounded. Shocked. And just about as excited as I'd ever been. It was love at first sight.

Oscar handed me a fly just like the one he was using. "Tie this on. It's called a Royal Wulff. The fly in my hand could best be described as strawberry shortcake for a fish. It was red and green with a slender brown tail and big white wings sticking up.

"That's called an attractor pattern. It doesn't really imitate a certain bug, but they go crazy for it up here."

We worked our way up the stream, learning to read the water, what a proper drift looked like, and casting to the likely spots. I hooked a lot of trees, tripped over a few slippery rocks, and scared a bunch of fish. Oscar just kept giving me tips and showing me how things worked. After a while, he left me on my own to perfect my skill.

That was Oscar. He taught me many things, but it never really felt like a lesson. More like a friend letting you in on what he knew. I'd have to say Oscar Cole was my first adult friend.

Don't get me wrong. I had other friends who were adults. But up to then they had all been both of those things – adults and friends. Oscar was a friend who just happened to be an adult. He treated me like an equal, let me pull my own weight, and laughed at me whenever he had the chance. Oscar thought he was pretty funny. Still does. (Did I mention that before?) He always took it as well as he gave it, though. And his teasing was always in fun.

One of our favorite jokes was to grade each other's falls when we were on the river. Fishing in a free-stone mountain stream full of mossy rocks can lead to a variety of gravitational disasters. We improved on the work of our favorite writer – Patrick F. McManus of *Outdoor Life* magazine- and created an elaborate scoring system for our falls, judging elements such as distance, overall wetness, scream quality and bodily injury. Oscar achieved a near perfect 9.85 out of a possible 10 one winter when I forced him to fish the 'Vacas during my college Christmas break. You see the ice he was standing on gave way and, well, it was a masterpiece.

Over the years, Oscar taught me more about how to read a stream, cast a fly, match the hatch, judge the weather and care for the river. He introduced me to magical places like the Guadalupe Box, The Rio De Los Pinos and Lagunitas. He taught me the art of fishing.

Oscar's friendship reminds me of something Jesus said to his disciples. It's recorded in John chapter 15, verse 15:

I do not call you slaves anymore, because a slave doesn't know what

his master is doing. I have called you friends, because I have made
known to you everything I have heard from My Father.

I have called you friends. Jesus elevated these lowly young
men to the lofty status, "Friend of God." He gave them
knowledge of his business. He taught them what he knew,
and passed on to them what had been entrusted to Him.
He treated them like friends, and their lives were forever
changed.

Notice what else Jesus said, "I have made known to you
everything I have heard from My Father." He didn't hold
out on them. He viewed them as worthy of everything he
had to offer. Because of this great gift - this great trust -
they were made powerful by His Spirit. They were
equipped for the task he gave them.

The gift Jesus gave those young men changed their lives,
but it didn't end there. They gave it away and others gave
it away, and on, and on, and on. Finally, the gift ended up
in the part of the world where I live, and was shared with
my family. We've decided it is best to keep passing it
along.

This gift Jesus gave his friends inspires and informs my
view of fishing. Fishing, for me, will always be a gift
because of three men whom I love, who gave it to me.
Just as Jesus gave his life to and for his friends; my Papa,
my Dad and my Friend gave fishing as a gift to me.

Over the last twenty-five years or so, I've had the chance
to give the gift as well. I taught my wife to fly-fish, and, to
varying degrees, each of my three daughters. I've taught
friends, and bosses, and travelling preachers to cast and to

catch. I've taken young men to the mountains and introduced them to my dear friend, fishing. And now that my oldest daughter has married, I've been able to share the gift with my son-in-law. I think we have some good times ahead of us.

A few years back, I took a group of young men to the Pecos wilderness. We hiked in four or five miles, and they all made fun of the old man and his creaking knees. We camped at a breathtaking spot called Mora Flats (no, the M doesn't sound like an H). We sat around the fire and talked about Jesus and life. We laughed and joked and made fun of each other. And in the morning, we fished.

One young man had never used a fly-rod, and wanted to learn. I spent a few minutes with him on basic casting, tied a hopper (that's a fly pattern that looks like a grasshopper) on the end of his leader, and headed upstream. I caught a couple while he watched, then we found a real nice hole. He seemed to want to do this mostly on his own, so I showed him where to cast, and moved up to the next hole.

After a few minutes I heard rustling in the brush and a voice broke my solitude. "Hey Rick, thanks for teaching me to fish!" I turned around and Thomas stood there grinning like a circus clown and holding a fat brown trout.

"You're welcome. Nice Job!" I replied. I whipped out my camera and took his picture with his first fly-caught trout. But all I could see in my mind's eye was Oscar Cole's taunting grin.

Gift given. Mission accomplished.

The desktop on my computer is a photo of me fly-fishing on Father's Day 2011 on the River Boyne in Ireland... a gift from my wife, and one of the favorite days of my life. In the picture, I'm casting across that beautiful Irish river with about thirty feet of line arcing in a perfect loop, guaranteed to raise a brown trout - real fishing magazine stuff. I think Papa, Dad and Oscar would all approve.

Now a few pages back, I made a promise to those of you who don't know what an improved clinch knot is: You don't tell anyone and I won't either. But I've got a better bargain for you. Let's go fishing, and I'll show you.

14 COACH

I believe for each of us, there are certain words that carry a greater meaning. Words that, when we hear them or say them, cause something to rise up inside us. Sure, there are the obvious ones, words like "mom" or "love" or "steak."

But for individual people, there are words that have that same effect – and no one else knows why. For me, one of those words is "coach."

I was raised by an athlete who was also a coach. My Dad excelled in sports all his life, and when he had three sons, he set out to teach them how to enjoy the sports he enjoyed. There were many sports played in our house, but football was king.

I remember standing in our front yard when I was six or seven years old, with a brother to my left and a brother to my right. Dad would hold a football, and without warning, throw it to one of us. Our job was to catch the ball properly – with our hands, not our chest. The fingers were spread apart, and the eyes were on the ball. All the way in.

Now please don't misunderstand. Dad wasn't one of those crazy "live my life through my kid" fanatics, who relentlessly drive their sons because dad doesn't have a life of his own. My dad always had a life of his own. He just wanted to share it with us.

As I grew up, I played football, tee-ball, baseball, basketball, tennis, golf, and a host of invented games that sprang from the fertile, destructive minds of my brothers and I. Some of our sports were played in a more organized fashion, which meant there would be a coach.

One of the earliest and most important lessons Dad taught us about playing on a team was how you treat your coach. The coach is the boss, and the players are to listen to the coach. The coach deserves your respect and full attention because he is your coach. Period.

The coach is also the one who decides your role on the team, so if you want to play, you'd better catch the coach's attention. If the coach says form a line here, you need to be the first one in line. If the coach says it is time to run, you'd better run as fast as you can. Listen to your coach, he knows what he's talking about. Obey your coach, he is in charge. Respect your coach, he is giving his time and effort for your good. And somewhere in that mix – for me at least - love your coach. Make him proud.

Over the years, I played for many coaches. Some were great, some were so-so, and some were not much. I remember one football team I played on where the coaches knew very little about football and almost nothing about young men. We went 0-7 that year, and only scored one touchdown (for the record, I scored that touchdown!).

After each defeat, the coaches would cuss and yell at us and subject us to endless windsprints and bear-crawls. If you don't know what bear-crawls are, be grateful.

When these two clowns would holler at us after a loss, they always threw in one important question. "Is it the coaches!?" They would yell. And I always wanted to respond.

"Of course it's the coaches! Who else would it be? You guys don't know what you're doing! The only thing you're good at is yelling and bullying kids. I could do a better job than you're doing, and I'm twelve!"

But I didn't. Now here's the part of the story where I'm going to surprise you. This isn't a story of abuse and pain. It isn't a story of my being scarred for life. Why? Because the reason I didn't yell back at the coaches was that I didn't have to. I would go home and talk to my Mom and Dad about those guys. My folks made sure I knew I was loved and secure, and they encouraged me to stick it out. Their love gave me the strength to stick it out.

You see the reality is this. It was a seven-game season. Three months out of my entire life. And the people whose love I knew at home made the rantings of a couple of Vince Lombardi wannabes very insignificant. Don't get me wrong. I didn't enjoy it, and I wouldn't want to do it again. But it wasn't the end of the world, and it helped me learn to deal with the hard things that are a part of every life.

As the years went by, I had some other coaches... some great ones. My favorite teacher in high school was a coach, though he never coached me. Mr. Carroll taught U.S. History and Economics at Belen High School. He was from Massachusetts, and he talked funny... sort of a John F. Kennedy meets John Wayne effect. He loved history, and he made it come alive. He also made students come alive.

I remember Mr. Carroll asking questions from our reading or for a test review. He'd throw out a question, and I'd raise my hand.

"Mr. Brittain!" When he said your name, it was like he was recognizing a member of Congress. "Expound, Mr. Brittain. Fill the room with knowledge!"

I always felt like the things that made Mr. Carroll a great teacher had a lot to do with his background as an athlete and a coach, combined with a love for learning. He taught as a form of coaching, and it worked.

As I mentioned, I never played football for Mr. Carroll, because at the beginning of my sophomore year, I decided to switch over to cross country. I had been running track for several years, and had come to love running. All of which brings me to my ultimate coach – the one man who, for me, will always be 'My Coach.'

I first met Phil Gregory at church when I was in sixth grade. His eldest son, Keith, and I were great friends as we grew through junior high and high school, and we spent a lot of time at one another's homes. Mr. Gregory was a cool guy, who always had time for his kids and their friends. He was funny, and had a great mustache (which was big in the 70s). I was vaguely aware that he taught at the high school and coached track.

During my freshman year, I became aware of Coach Gregory in a new way. He was the head track coach at BHS, and I suddenly found myself on his team. On his team was a good place to be.

As I've mentioned before, I was never a great athlete, but I have always loved sports. I think I love track more than any team sport. Football and basketball are easy to watch and follow, and I enjoy them plenty. But there's something about track and field for me that is pure and genuine. It is sport at its most basic. The sights and sounds and smells of a track meet do something magical for me, and I think coach Gregory has a lot to do with that.

He was the first coach who ever really taught me the deeper things of a sport: anatomy, kinetics, physiology, recovery, technique. He explained to me why he set up workouts the way he did, what he hoped to achieve with certain athletes, and what body types were best for certain events. He helped me learn what was a good time for a certain event, and how to judge progress in a runner.

If you wonder why I got the opportunity to learn all those things, it is because I spent much of my track and cross-country career walking around with the coach, writing numbers on a clip-board or helping him tape other people's ankles. I was always hurt, so I had to find other ways to contribute to the team!

Don't feel too bad for the team, though. You see, I was a below average pole-vaulter and high-jumper, a terrible

hurdler, a slow sprinter and a middle of the pack distance
runner. On the other hand, I could rub Kramer's or
Atomic Balm into a calf muscle with the best of them, so I
did my part.

And I watched. I watched coach Gregory mold young
men into runners. I watched him schedule workouts so
the team would peak at just the right time. I watched him
get the most out of the guys. And in all this watching, I
learned a whole lot about what it means to influence
people.

A coach is an influencer. He or she takes the raw material
of a group of young athletes and forms a team. A coach
helps individuals find out what they have inside them, and
then draws it out. They build players and out of players
build teams, and in the process build men and women who
will go on to become influencers of others. That's what
coaches do, and I love them for it.

That's why for me, coach is a word with deep meaning. It
carries weight, and it carries honor. Because of who I am
and where I came from, it is one of the greatest
compliments I can ever give. If I call you coach, and one
of my kids isn't playing on your team, it means
something... something good.

The greatest coach in the Bible was Jesus himself, but
another of my favorites is a guy named Paul, who I've
mentioned before. Paul used quite a few sports metaphors
in his writing. It appears he may have been a runner or a
boxer, or both in his day. In one of Paul's letters to his
favorite student-athlete (Timothy), Paul says this,

"And what you have heard from me in the presence of many witnesses, commit to faithful men who will be able to teach others also." 2 Timothy 2:2

What Paul was telling Timothy is the same thing Jesus told his followers, and us, in Matthew 28:18-20:

"All authority has been given to Me in heaven and on earth. Go, therefore, and make disciples of all nations, baptizing them in the name of the Father and of the Son and of the Holy Spirit, teaching them to observe everything I have commanded you. And remember, I am with you always, to the end of the age."

"Teach them what I have taught you." It's one thing to coach, but my favorite coaches were the ones like Phil Gregory, who taught more than how to play the game. He taught me what the game was, and how it worked, and gave me understanding that would make other lives better.

Another great thing about learning from coach Gregory was that I also got to learn from his mentor – coach Gardner, and from *his* mentor – coach Burke. Right before my eyes were three generations of coaches passing the baton to the next generation.

The life of a Christ-follower is like that. It is to be learned and taught. Make no mistake, Jesus is the teacher. He is the focal point, and He is the only one who can save. But he invites those who learn from him to teach others what they have learned.

If you are a disciple of Jesus, you should be learning –

from someone. Every player needs a coach. Even Peyton Manning needs a coach. Do you have a coach? Who are you learning from?

If you are a disciple of Jesus, you should be coaching – someone. Every coach needs a player. Even John Wooden (greatest coach ever) needed a team on the court. Do you have a player? Who are you influencing?

The reality of passing it on came home for me a few years back when I was asked to coach at a local high school. I had friends coaching track at the school, and I was helping with the *Fellowship of Christian Athletes* huddle group there, so I thought I'd go by track practice and watch the kids suffer.

I said hi to some people, laughed at the young hurdlers a bit, and headed over to the pole-vault area. I struck up a conversation with the frustrated coach who, it turned out, was a brilliant hurdling coach, but didn't have much knowledge or interest in the field of pole-vaulting. When he found out I knew a little bit, and loved the sport, he took me over to see the head coach.

"Hey Joe," he said, "I found us a pole-vault coach."

So with permission from my pastor over at the church where I was working, and a certification course at the State High School Athletic Association, I found myself a volunteer track coach.

Now pole vault is an interesting sport. I think it is the ultimate sport. It requires speed, strength, flexibility, coordination, technique, focus and immense courage. If any of these elements are missing, you are simply out of luck. If pole-vault were easy, they'd call it football.

We had several vaulters, both male and female, with varying degrees of skill, experience and insanity (which is a basic tenet of pole-vault). There was one young man in particular, who the coaches had high hopes for. The head coach needed some points at the State Championships from this guy, and it became my job to find them.

Josh had suffered a series of knee injuries, so he wasn't good for too many vaults in a row. He had the speed and the strength and all the other elements – including the courage. He just didn't have too many reps in the tank, if you know what I mean. Josh was also just a bit of a head-case, which almost every pole-vaulter is.

As I began working with Josh, I identified a few areas for improvement, most of which had to do with his head, and not his body. We got some thought processes worked out, got control of some temper, and tweaked a few techniques. Josh won the district meet and was one of the top seeds by the time we got to State.

As usual, Josh waited to come in until the bar was at 13 feet. He cleared 13 on his first attempt, and 13'6" on his second. Now the bar rested at 14 feet, and there were only two vaulters left. They both missed the fist and second attempts, and Josh's opponent missed his third.

Final attempt at 14 feet. If he clears, he wins. If he misses, he finishes second on a tie-break technicality. I was nervous, but I tried to hide it. I shouted the brilliant words of encouragement coaches say at a moment like that when they know they have absolutely nothing to do with the outcome, but I stayed out of Josh's way. My part in the game was over, and this was Josh's day. Win or lose, I was proud of him, and so grateful to have shared his journey.

I got out of the way and started pacing back and forth while Josh got set up. I was giddy, and certainly looked a little bit ridiculous. I found out how ridiculous as Josh cleared the bar to win the State Championship.

I jumped, screaming my delight, landed, spun around and threw my hat toward the fence. As I ran over to retrieve the hat, I looked up and saw all the other coaches – the real coaches who worked at the school and got paid to be out here – smiling and laughing at me. They were thrilled for Josh and for the team, but they were just plain cracked up at me.

I walked over with a sheepish grin on my face, ready to take the ribbing I had coming. The head-man just looked up at me and said, "Congratulations, coach."

Nice. He called me coach. I can live with that.

It has been a few years since I coached a sport, but I get to spend a lot of time these days coaching young men and women in matters of faith, and the same principles hold true. There's nothing like watching one of my vaulters clear a height for the first time, or mastering a technique. But even better is watching someone clear a challenge in life by faith or master the art of passing the Gospel story on to someone they care about.

Jesus said it like this, *"The harvest is plentiful, but the workers are few."* The Kingdom of God needs coaches.

15 FALLING IN LOVE

I looked into the most beautiful green eyes God ever made and heard the words I'd been longing for.

"So if it's okay with you, I'd like to start over, as friends, and see what happens."

I looked back into those green eyes, so happy that I would have another chance. So happy that she was interested in me again. So happy.

My thoughts of happiness were interrupted by a voice speaking a single word.

"No."

I heard the voice, recognized it, and realized it was mine.

How do you arrive at a frozen-in-time moment? A moment where your whole life and future hang in the balance? How do you land in a moment where you're willing to risk everything you've dreamed of, because you know that if you mess this up, nothing will ever be the same again? Here's how it happened to me.

Growing up in Belen, I never had much interaction with girls. I liked girls, but they didn't seem to have a whole lot of time for me. Girls made me nervous.

It didn't help that my big brother was a girl-magnet. He always had a girlfriend. My younger brother, David, and I were always laughing at Mike, making fun of his cologne and his cool shirts, and how he was always wasting his money on girls. I thought this was all very funny until I realized girls were kind of interesting and pretty. They smelled nice, and began to seem more and more worthwhile.

I just never seemed to have the talent with girls that Mike did. I even had a sort of girlfriend that informed me she'd rather spend time with my brother than with me. Ouch. I never told him about that, so keep a lid on it for me.

Anyway, as the years went by, I did manage a girlfriend or two. I solved the mystery a bit during my first two years in college. I dated two or three girls in Texas, but nothing really came of it.

Half way through my third year, I had to move back home to Belen. I needed to sort out some things about what I was going to do with my life, instead of changing majors every semester, so I moved home and got a job. I helped out quite a bit at church, and waited to see what was going to happen.

Meanwhile, David had discovered girls as well. Actually, he only discovered one girl. They started hanging out together at church, and the next thing you know they've been married twenty-eight years. I'm pretty sure neither of them ever went on a date with anyone besides each other. Impressive.

So now Mike is married (to his first sweetheart from way back in middle school, by the way), David has found the love of his life on the first try, and Mom and Dad are getting a little worried about the awkward middle child.

I know they were worried because Dad kept trying to set me up. Daughters of friends, girls at church, you name it. One day we went to lunch and he tried to set me up with the waitress. I'm still not sure I wasn't part of the tip.

So imagine my terror when I arrived at the camp and heard my friend Oscar say those words, "he's at it again."

Dad and the kids from our church youth choir were at Inlow Youth Camp, in the Manzano Mountains for the week. Several other friends of mine from around New Mexico were there as well, and I thought it might be fun to spend my day off going up for a visit.

When Oscar told me dad was at it again, I almost got back in my pickup to drive home, but then Oscar set the hook. "This one's worth checking out." He snickered to himself and walked away.

Now I could see it. My Dad and my best fishing buddy were in this together. There was no way I could get out of this, and that look in Oscar's eye told me I probably didn't want to.

It was lunch time, so I walked into the cafeteria to say hi. I saw Dad across the room and walked over. We hugged, said hello, and then he lit up. "Hey, there's somebody I want you to meet!"

He led me over to the lunch line - the moment of truth. I heard the theme from 'Jaws" playing in my head. He stopped in front of a girl, and I looked up. I had a few thoughts in rapid succession.

First, I had to spend a second on the girl. Did I mention those green eyes? Wow. And the face. Spectacular. I began to be pretty sure I'd seen her on television at some point. This girl was amazing.

Now I was always a sucker for brunettes. When all my buddies had crushes on Farah Fawcett, I was hung up on Jaclyn Smith. I liked Mary Ann better than Ginger, and Wonder Woman owned my heart.

That was it! She looked like Wonder Woman, only younger, and much prettier.

Which brings me to my second thought. In that moment, I despised my Dad. How could he try to set me up with a girl that far out of my league? Didn't he know how much this would hurt me? I shook her hand, mumbled a few words of greeting and small talk, and walked away. Sure, I was hung up on her. That crush happened in a heartbeat. But a man's got to know his limitations. I didn't figure to waste my time on high hopes and heartbreak, so I made my escape.

After lunch I walked around for a while and talked to a

few friends, but the reasons for my visit to that camp had changed without my permission. All I could think about was the girl. Finally, I decided that if I was going to be miserable anyway, I might as well have a reason. I would talk to her. I found out later that she wanted to talk to me as well, despite my rudeness in the lunch line.

We managed to run into each other, and spent the rest of the day together. We had a great time. I found out she didn't think she was too good for me after all. By the time I started my car to drive home that night, I knew the name of the woman I would marry. I am not making this up. I was through with females that weren't Kris Wendland.

I guess deciding I was going to marry her got me over my fears, because the next time I saw her, on our first real date, I kissed her goodnight. Over the next few months we spent as much time together as we could. We met each other's families, and we both burned up the highway between Albuquerque and Phoenix, where Kris went to school.

One night, in the driveway in front of her parents' house, I said the words to her that I had vowed I would say to only one woman in my life. "I love you." I wasn't talking about family love or Christian love or friendship love. I was talking about "I think you're the greatest girl on the planet and I want to spend the rest of my life with you" love. And yes, she said she loved me too.

Paradise lasted a few more weeks, then strange things started happening. She didn't answer when I called, didn't return my calls or answer my letters (this was before cell phones and texting kids – the dark ages). Then one night she told me she wanted to date other people, that the long-distance thing wasn't working out.

"You're not doing this over the phone," I said. "I want to see you face to face."

We agreed to meet when Kris came home for Thanksgiving break, and I held out hope. Maybe she'd change her mind. Maybe she would realize what a great guy I was. Maybe not.

We sat in a restaurant and stared at our plates for a half hour without a word. Finally, I subtly broke the ice. "Well?"

"Well," she said, "Like I told you on the phone..." and she let me down easy. I really don't remember anything she said that night, because she didn't say yes.

I drove her back home, dropped her off, and headed forward into my life of misery and loneliness. I was pitiful. I listened to nothing but country music for three solid months. George Strait was my only friend. I cried and moped. I was pathetic. Then a really cool thing happened.

I decided it was time to see if Jesus could help me out with this mess. I started praying and serving more. I invested in other people. I remembered what God wanted me to do with my life, and I started pursuing that.

Within a few months, I had left my retail sales job and was serving at a small church in Grants, New Mexico. I came back to life, and found my purpose again. This was good.

In July, I found myself back at that same camp where I'd

met Kris the year before. I hadn't really thought about seeing her there again... Okay, that's a lie. I had thought about little else for a good while before the camp started.

And see her, I did. Within an hour of arriving at Inlow, there was a huge rainstorm, and Kris and I wound up under the same shelter, with about thirty other people. Awkward.

I had tried to convince myself that I didn't need her anymore; that I'd be fine without her. I even told my friend Oscar later that day that she wasn't really all that great, and I didn't know why I had been so overboard about her. I managed to make it through the day without falling apart, but it was touch and go.

I don't remember whether it was Monday evening, or Tuesday evening, but at some point, Kris ran into my Mom, and asked if she knew where I was. The text of my Mother's response remains a mystery, but I guess it ran somewhere along the lines of "If you hurt my son again, I'll rip your lips off."

It seems Kris had been thinking about me, as well. She finally found me and suggested we go somewhere quiet and have a talk. I was terrified, but willing. Kind of like a bungee jumper right before the big moment.

We walked to the camp chapel, went inside and sat down on a pew. Kris proved she was nervous as well (a good sign in my book), by repeatedly assuring me that she "wasn't expecting anything from me." I kept asking her what she wanted from me.

This circular discussion went on for a while, then Kris let me know she felt it would be a good idea if we "started over as friends." We would then see how things went, and go from there. Tidy, clean, risk free. Perfect.

But it wasn't perfect, and I think we both knew it. I knew I could no more be just her friend than I could have a passing acquaintance with oxygen. I had already given my heart to this woman. It was too late for friendship.

"No," said the voice that turned out to be mine. "Either you commit to me, or this won't work."

The funny thing about these big moments in life – and all moments, I guess – is that there are two people in the conversation, with their own thoughts, known only to themselves.

When I said, "commit to me", I meant "enter an important relationship with me, and let's see if we have a future together – which I desperately hope we do."

What Kris heard was, "Marry me." I learned recently that agreeing to my wobbly ultimatum, in her mind, meant she was agreeing to be my wife.

We sat in silence for a few seconds, which felt like a few years, and then she said the most important word ever uttered in a human relationship in my life. Actually, it wasn't a word, it was two letters:

"Ok."

And with the utterance of those two little letters, everything in my life changed for the better.

As I write this, we've lived the adventure together for over twenty-seven years. She has loved me, taught me, humbled me and brought the spice to my life. Outside eternity -which is sort of a big deal - she is the best gift God has ever given me.

We have three daughters, the oldest of whom got married in the summer of 2014. Like her Mom, Haylee married a preacher boy who has a lot to learn. She's a brilliant hairdresser and homemaker, sings like a bird, believes in sharing her faith with people she cares for, and she is an influencer in the lives of many young women.

Our second daughter, Mattelynn graduated from high school a year early, and is off at college preparing for a life somewhere in Africa. She plans to invest herself in kids who have no family, and teach the gospel of Jesus to a world that desperately needs Him.

Our youngest, Sydney, is still figuring life out, but she's a fine actress and a shining example of what a disciple looks like – and she's off to college to learn about Biblical languages or some such nonsense. She also knows how to handle several different kinds of swords, so don't mess with her. Amazing.

I mention these three because the biggest reason for their success in life is that Jesus gave them Kris Wendland-Brittain as a mother, a model and a mentor. They are the fruit of her faith, beauty, wisdom and love. They are her trophies, and I am the beneficiary of the whole package. Wonder Woman couldn't carry this girl's purse.

So boys, let me give you a piece of advice. When God drops a raven-haired beauty with piercing green eyes and a face you could stare at for the rest of your days into your path, muster up a little courage… it just might pay off in the end.

ABOUT THE AUTHOR

Rick Brittain and his wife, Kris have served churches in New Mexico, Texas, Arizona and Tennessee. Rick currently serves the Baptist Convention of New Mexico as Regional Missionary for Northern NM. This allows him to spend time investing in men and fly-fishing on the side… an arrangement that proves God is very kind.

Rick hopes this book will help men, and others, to know the Savior better, and understand something new about the life He offers each of us.

John Muir said, "The mountains are calling and I must go." King David of Bethlehem said,

I lift my eyes to the mountains. Where will my help come from? My help comes from the Lord, the maker of heaven and earth. Psalm 121:1-2

Rick agrees with both of them!

Printed in Great Britain
by Amazon